12,000 Miles of Road Thoughts. Old Van, Old Man, Recovering Hippie, Dying Cat

PAUL WILLCOTT

Published by Wordstruck Press, 2023.

12,000 MILES OF ROAD THOUGHTS. OLD VAN, OLD MAN, RECOVERING HIPPIE, DYING CAT

First edition. June 26, 2023.

ISBN: 979-8215493144

Written by PAUL WILLCOTT.

Also by PAUL WILLCOTT

Annals of Franklin Manor
A Franklin Manor Christmas
A Franklin Manor Epiphany

Standalone
12,000 Miles of Road Thoughts. Old Van, Old Man, Recovering
Hippie, Dying Cat
In Passing. Scenes from an Unconventional Life

Watch for more at paulwillcott.com.

Table of Contents

CHAPTER ONE
ROADSIDE ASSISTANCE

When the alarm sounds at 4:00 a.m., the Austin temperature is seventy-five and the humidity, 91%. It's the kind of morning when my Okie grandmother would say, "It's gonna be a scorcher," and she would be right. She was always right when she said that. It will reach a hundred or so before we get to New Mexico at the end of the day.

For the better part of three hours, we lug gear down two flights of stairs and pack the inside of the van and climb the ladder to stuff the rooftop luggage carrier. We are soaked with sweat before we're well started. We let the air conditioning run for the last half hour before leaving so Baby Kitty, aka BK, won't have to wait for it to cool down after we start. She's sick, we're going to be on the road for weeks, and we want at least this first day to go well.

Finally, I put the van in gear, point it in the direction of Lopez Island in Puget Sound, and go.

Austin is the state capital. Politicians who dislike Austin drive in from rural areas every two years and do their cussedest to thwart the city's progressive tendencies. Liberalism aside, Austin is defined by country music, Longhorn football, sprawl, and choking traffic.

The van is well suited to stop-and-go driving; in such conditions, we don't hold up the flow. But when we leave on Saturday morning, traffic on the highway out of town is light; road rage and boredom are replaced by NASCAR moves. Wannabe racecar drivers choking on backed-up testosterone tailgate at high speed and switch lanes for the fun of it. We stay on access roads as much as possible and accept red lights as our fate.

After an hour or so, we emerge from the suburbs, and the highway narrows to a more human scale – two lanes with intermittent stretches of three lanes to accommodate passing. Between passing lanes, we push the speed, so we won't be in the way of pickup drivers with their Second Amendment and anti-choice bumper stickers. It's a good bet they are already boiling angry without getting held up by a classic VW van, which to them symbolizes much that's causing America to lose its way.

My sense of being in hostile territory notwithstanding, the surrounding countryside is welcoming in a way. Gently rolling hills are decorated with low growths of cedar, mesquite, and cactus, which do fine in the smelter-level heat. Despite parched soil and rattlesnakes and cactus, it's a quiet, even pacific, vista.

Passing through this country calls up my unshakeable ambivalence toward Texas. Not since I was in grade school have I been able to come down totally on one side of the love-hate divide. It's a burden. I doubt it would be so uncomfortable to have mixed feelings about, say, Kansas or Nevada, but the life force of Texas is so strong it allows no half measures. All-or-nothing thinking is in the air Texans breathe. George Bush famously announced a foreign policy based on "you're either for us or against us." (I suppose we should be grateful he didn't just abolish the State Department.)

The first town we come to is Lampasas, population 7900. The county it's located in has twenty-five people per square mile. The next county, Mills, has seven people per square mile, and a total population of 4791. It voted 87% for Trump in 2016. We are entering a way of being far removed from Democratic Austin with its world-class university and a growth rate of 152 people a day. It's only seventy miles behind us.

We pass through Lometa, population 845. According to worldpopulationreview.com, it's the 857th largest "city" in Texas.

By now, the sun is directly overhead, and the temperature is rising to a searing August-in-Texas level. The oil-temperature gauge registers a similar increase, so to keep the engine from overheating, we turn off the air conditioning. I try not to think about having paid $2000 for an AC system we can't use when the weather is hot.

Ten or fifteen miles past Lometa, it's time for a break so the engine can cool off a little and we can stretch our legs. A roadside park comes into view. It's not much of one, though, just a patch of brown stubble surrounding a couple of concrete picnic tables under a plastic shed roof. Being out of the sun will help a little, but the breeze is hot. That's unfortunate; as it turns out, we are there all afternoon.

As I ease onto the gravel at the edge of the road, the engine dies. I turn the key and crank the engine repeatedly. No response. It's all too familiar; probably vapor locked like when Joe Rodriguez, the man with the chain, and Jimmy, the born-again wrecker driver, rescued me. Oh well, I've been to that rodeo. I can handle it.

At some point, the vaporized fuel will turn back into liquid, the engine will start, and by driving very slowly with flashers flashing, we can make it to one of those nice air-conditioned Dairy Queens or Subways that even the smallest towns have, and we'll slug down some iced tea and figure out what to do next. Maybe we'll stay till sundown when even in Texas the temperature drops some and resume our trip in the dark. Back when lots of cars, even those with water-cooled engines, overheated in summer, people would cross Death Valley or the Mojave Desert at night. Or maybe we'll check into a motel, watch some tv, have a drink or two, and start again very early the next morning.

I keep turning the key, each time hoping and each time being disappointed. The battery is new, so I can do that for a long time without running it down. It's still going strong when Ann and I and Baby Kitty begin to run down.

We had sweated buckets while loading, and excited to get the adventure started, we forgot to camel up before starting. We haven't even brought much water with us. We would have gotten some in Lampasas, if we had stopped to pee, but we were too dried out to have the urge. When the engine quit, we were drinking the last few swallows we had.

We saved enough to fill Baby Kitty's bowl, but she won't drink. That is her way when traveling; she won't eat or drink or use her litter box. When flying or taking long trips, we welcome that. Not in this case, though. Her kidneys are failing; it's a bad time for her to refuse water.

She lies on the floor, her mouth open a little, breathing rapidly. We leave the side door open and point a small battery-powered fan in her direction. It blows hot air. Her ribs show noticeably. She's skinnier than we had realized. Is this trip going to ask too much of her? We had thought about that beforehand, but just when she didn't seem up to it, she would play and carry on the same as always. Every morning when I took Ann wake-up coffee, she would follow me into the bedroom, jump onto the bed, make herself comfortable on Ann's breast, and look "Good Morning" into her eyes. Right up till shortly before starting, lab tests showed her to be holding up well. Statistically, her chances of living longer than the trip would take were excellent. But lying on the floor of the van, Ann beside her and petting her while the temperature continues to rise, she looks like we might have made a dreadful mistake.

Before long, Ann and I get so thirsty we realize we're going to be in trouble if we go much longer without water. How could we have been so reckless? We knew what Texas summer is like. Water is essential if you're traveling in remote areas. I'm not even sure exactly where we are.

I go as far out on the road as I dare and stick out my thumb. There is little traffic, and for a while, what few cars and trucks there are whoosh by without slowing down.

Eventually, one turns around and comes back. Its hood is partly open, and its engine is coughing and sputtering. The driver is sweating heavily, the car's air conditioning obviously not working.

"Hello. Could you give me a ride to the next town so I can get some water? My van has broken down, and we've run out."

Without saying anything, she swings her right arm over to the passenger side in the movement everybody's mother used before there were seat belts to keep a child in place when suddenly braking. She brings it back with a one-gallon plastic jug of water in her hand. There are several more on the seat.

"I'll stay with you until you get help."

I can't say for sure how old she is. In her thirties, I guess. She's wearing tattered flannel pajamas with a good-sized hole in one knee. She follows me over to the van and says hello to Ann and strokes BK and talks kitty talk to her.

Her name is Cindy. She keeps several gallons of water on the seat by her so she can fill the boiling-over radiator of the Pontiac, which she bought for $300. Her husband knows how to fix it, but he never gets around to it. She seems to accept that in him. She's on her way to a town up the road called Mullin, population 178, for a weekend visit with her young daughter who lives there with Cindy's mother and sister.

"Do you believe in angels?" I ask.

"Sure," she says.

"Me too," I say.

"Me too," Ann says.

That settles the question of who she is and why she has showed up with water. But in worn *flannel* pajamas in August in a broken-down wreck of a car?

Thinking about it later, I recall what I heard Presbyterian preachers say on just about every Sunday of my boyhood. "The Lord moves in mysterious ways, His wonders to perform." It hadn't meant much to me at the time.

CHAPTER TWO
BEEN THERE, DONE THAT – SORT OF

This attempt at a long, carefree drive out west was beginning to seem too much like an earlier adventure with an unreliable vehicle.

In the late 1960s, I was one of twenty American lecturers at the University of Baghdad. We were employees of the University of Texas, which had been contracted to manage the Fulbright program for Iraq. I would not have been part of the program except that Austin badly wanted my then wife to be onsite administrator, and to get her meant taking me (a graduate student with a spotty academic record) and our five-year-old son. As part of our compensation, we got a 1967 Chevrolet station wagon complete with Texas license plates, air conditioning, a triptyque that allowed us to cross international borders without incurring customs charges, and after a time, a driver. It was a perk of mixed benefits.

The station wagon ran faultlessly when I drove the 935 miles from the dealership in Beirut over the Lebanese mountains through Damascus and across the Iraqi desert, but soon after arriving in Baghdad, an electrical problem began a nasty habit of eating the battery. Sometimes it was too weak to start the engine. Sometimes the lights would go out – while we were driving. On its face, that would seem easy to remedy: just replace the alternator, check wiring all around, that sort of thing. But I never got closer to proper repair than a shrug and a theory that the six-cylinder engine was not powerful enough to support air conditioning. (At the time, air-conditioned cars were unusual in Iraq,) We didn't use the air conditioning for a while.

Not surprisingly, it affected nothing. But we just kept driving it and accepting the inconvenience of breakdowns until I sold it two years later.

One breakdown was more than inconvenient, it was life-threatening. On a holiday trip, we were ascending in the dark the pass through the ten-thousand-foot mountains between Damascus and Beirut, when light snow turned blindingly heavy. At the same time, headlights and dash lights failed. Even when the headlights were still working, it was hard to see either the center line or the guard rail on the right; without lights, they were invisible. Beyond the guard rail, the ground fell away steeply to a depth known only to Allah.

There was little traffic other than the occasional heavy truck, but even so, stopping seemed more dangerous than slowly continuing. A friend who was with us stuck his head out of the passenger window and did his best to warn me when I got close to the guard rail. When trucks came up behind us, we held our breath but were grateful for the brief help of their headlights. Eventually, we reached the crest and made our way down to the border crossing where we got help.

Problems with the station wagon were not limited to mechanical issues. His first day on the job, Abbas, a driver employed by the program, hit a blind man. I was at home grading papers, when he arrived with the victim and the boy who served as his eyes in the back seat. The man was unhurt, and if Iraq had tort lawyers, they didn't get involved, so nothing further came of the incident.

Abbas did have one moment of notable valor. It probably saved my life.

When the Six Day War was starting in early June, 1967, angry mobs filled the streets. In the minds of many Iraqis, the Israeli enemy and the United States were one, and as tensions grew, a mob stormed down the street in front of our house on their way to burn the American library a few blocks away.

That evening, I had to run an errand. I've forgotten what, but it must have been important. On the way, Abbas inadvertently drove the bright white Chevrolet station wagon with Texas license plates into the outer perimeter of a raging mob. He yelled at me to get down on the floor in the back and make myself as small as possible, instruction I didn't need. He made a tire-squealing U-turn and got me home safely.

The next day, all "unofficial Americans" (there were many in addition to the professors in the Texas program) were advised to assemble at the embassy for safe conduct to Iran, which at the time, was an American ally. Diplomatic relations between Iraq and the United States were being severed, civil unrest was growing, and there was fear of attack by the Israelis. We were not required to evacuate, but to stay in Iraq after the embassy was shuttered was a risk we were not ready to take.

We spent the day anxiously packing and saying goodbye to University colleagues who came by and braved the security police in front of our house. When the time came, we got in the heavily loaded Chevrolet and drove through the city and over the Tigris River to the embassy. Abbas declined to drive us, but another Iraqi who worked for the Texas program rode along and directed us through quiet back streets. He stayed with us until it became likely he would be seen in the Americans' big car. As it turned out, he was arrested after we evacuated and charged with being a *jasus* (spy) because he had worked for us.

While waiting for the evacuation to start, the embassy staff who weren't busy destroying documents took names and gave directions. After a bit, an official called us to order and made some announcements. Then the Belgian ambassador, who was going to manage Iraqi-American affairs going forward, was introduced. He told a moving story that brought many of us to tears. He had been a young boy in occupied Belgium during World War II, when one ordinary war-shaped day, he watched the sky fill with American paratroopers. He was deeply grateful for this opportunity to help us out. He said

– more likely, I heard it later – that the American government had asked Tunisia and Switzerland to take over management of American interests, but both had declined. The Belgian had accepted without bothering to consult Brussels.

Buses were provided for those who needed transportation, and at around midnight a long line of vehicles left the embassy under the protection of a heavily armed military escort.

The sun was coming up as we arrived at the international border. On the Iranian side, an American official greeted us. Somewhat farther on, we stopped at an Iranian Air Force base where we were put up in a sort of dormitory for bachelor officers, which was oddly unoccupied. We rested there until the following morning. In Tehran, we were led to a reception facility at the American embassy (the one which would be taken over by militants twelve years later) and given food and aid as needed.

In Baghdad, we had felt a strong sense of purpose and took pleasure in our work. And though diplomatic relations between the United States and Iraq had been severed, actual fighting had not come to Iraq. So, my family and I waited in Tehran for most of the summer, hoping for permission to return. It was not to be.

We had enough money to drive to somewhere in Europe, and for reasons I can't remember, we thought Rome would be a good place to stop and figure out what to do with our lives and the station wagon. We were young, imprudent, foolish, brash, adventuresome, and naive; the long trip there in an unreliable vehicle didn't figure in our thinking.

Northwest of Tehran, we crossed a desert where there was no road, only numerous tracks on hard-packed sand. We didn't have a compass, but now and then, a long-haul truck driver working the route between India and Europe would wave to us to follow him. The electrical system held up through the crossing, but the station wagon did develop an alarming clunking sound when going over a bump.

After a night in a sleazy hostel in Tabriz, we entered Turkey. We stopped for lunch in a small town, and before parking on the street, I looked around for someone I could hire to keep an eye on the station wagon and the gear on the luggage rack. A young boy who had learned some English from a Peace Corps teacher accepted eagerly. I gave him some money, but I think he might have done it for nothing.

After lunch, the car would not start, and the boy continued to help us. He found a garage to work on the car, then took us to his uncle's hazelnut farm to wait. We spent the afternoon drinking tea with the family and being taught how to play backgammon.

The garage got the car started but was unable to fix the clunking sound. It was diagnosed as a cracked chassis, and that was beyond their capability. I tried to get it fixed later in Istanbul and other places, but I never found anyone who could do it. Every time the clunk sounded, it alarmed me, but no serious harm ever came from it.

We drove on across Turkey and Greece and almost into Italy before we had another problem. When the ferry docked at Brindisi and the ramp went down, the battery was dead. We were near the front of a long line, and the ferry was huge. A deafening amount of honking and yelling rose up behind us. Seeing the Texas license plates, an Italian guy who had lived in Houston emerged from back in the line and took control. He got another car to push the station wagon off the ferry and get us going fast enough so that I could start the engine by slipping the clutch with it in gear. It was one of several times I was glad the dealer did not have a car with an automatic transmission. Another breakdown and another temporary reprieve occurred before we got to Rome.

During the evacuation, when we crossed the border into Iran, the American official who greeted us handed us some walking-around money in Iranian rials, no questions asked, no papers signed. I can't remember how much. It was a peculiarly American way to be a refugee. So was the refugee camp where some of us stayed – the Tehran Hilton.

In addition, the official covered the first page of our passports with a large stamp that read "NOT VALID FOR TRAVEL TO IRAQ" and other Muslim countries. That did not lessen our desire to go back, and we were still thinking of returning when we got to Rome in August. Our fear of being in Iraq with no embassy to rely on had lessened in the time since we had evacuated, so I went to the Iraqi Embassy and asked for a visa. The stamp in my passport meant nothing to the Iraqi clerk nor to me, and I was soon on a plane back. My wife, son, and the Chevrolet remained in Rome until I could see how it was in Baghdad.

The house we had lived in was still leased to the Texas program and a caretaker had looked after it in our absence. Word of my presence traveled fast. In the short time between getting off the plane and taking a taxi to the house, a number of Iraqis gathered there. They were mostly domestic workers who had been employed by Americans. They thought my return meant that all the Americans were coming back, or if not that, perhaps I would hire them. They were wrong.

To my knowledge there were only two other Americans in the country at the time – a man who worked for a nongovernmental organization, and an administrative officer from the embassy staff. He had remained behind to keep an eye on the building, including the contents of its commissary. He was glad to have my company, and we spent a few weeks palling around under the watchful eye of security police, enjoying U.S. government steaks and whisky.

I took it upon myself to approach the president of the University and ask if he would like to resume the Texas program. Of course, he did. Twenty professors at no cost was a swell gift, never mind diplomatic niceties. He did not have the authority to authorize it, though, so he picked up his phone and called the Prime Minister. After a short conversation, he told me the program could resume.

I was proud of myself, real proud. This diplomacy business was easier than the foreign service would have people believe. The Texas program was back in business, and it was because I had taken direct action and like a good salesman, asked for the order. I soon learned, however, that the State Department would have to agree to it, even though it was nominally a University of Texas program. I went to work on it, with a twenty-eight-year old's zeal.

I was allowed to communicate with Austin by cable from the former American ambassador's residence, which then was occupied by an aristocratic young Belgian named Vilan XIV and his bikini-clad girlfriend who seemed always to be lolling by the pool.

I sent repeated cables to the University of Texas representative who was trying to persuade Washington to go along with the agreement the young professor had so deftly negotiated. The State Department would not hear of it.

I did get a sort of consolation prize for my efforts – a teaching position in Amman at the University of Jordan. During the year we were there, I had the Chevrolet shipped from Rome. I drove it around town and sightseeing in surrounding areas, dealing with the continuing electrical problem, always administering temporary fixes, never finding the cause, and never getting the alarming clunk fixed.

In addition, I added body work by t-boning the personal car of the Amman Chief of Police. No one was hurt, and the damage was not extreme, but the Chief was angry. Showing insurance, license, and title was insufficient to keep us from being taken to the police station. We were not mistreated, though, and the American consul showed up after a bit, said whatever it is consuls say in such situations, and we were released.

Near the end of the academic year, I sold the station wagon to an American who worked for AID. I must have given him an excellent price because I made no secret of the vehicle's shortcomings. I lost touch of the guy afterward, and I've wondered from time to time what became of the car. Maybe it's better not to know. In any case, its revenant shows up on the side of the Texas road between Lometa and Mullin while we wait for help.

Eventually, it becomes clear that the van is not going to revive anytime soon. We call AAA, and with that, Cindy feels free to leave us. We embrace, and she chugs off in her dying Pontiac.

While waiting for the wrecker, a man in a car with Colorado plates stops to check on us. Then another man in a heavy-duty pickup pulling a livestock trailer stops. Neither of them can help in a practical way. They do reinforce what Cindy has given us – the sense that we aren't alone in the world.

At 4:00, a wrecker operated by a man named Billy Murphy arrives from his home about thirty miles away. We climb up into the cab of the Kenworth, and he drives Ann, BK, me, and the van back to Austin. BK revives quickly riding on Ann's lap in front of a working air-conditioning vent.

We chat during the two-hour drive but take care to avoid any subject that is even borderline political. Chances are we would disagree, perhaps angrily.

Billy is tired. He works 24/7, and he's been answering distress calls since before daylight. Nevertheless, when we get to Motormania, the Austin garage, it's closed, and he, like Cindy, won't leave us till someone comes to take us the remaining fifteen or so miles to our condo.

After an hour or so, a taxi driven by a man with the angel's name, Uriel, arrives. His lovely fourth-grade daughter, Sophia, is with him. Uriel is proprietor of a one-taxi company. Like Billy, he works all the time, including this Saturday night. He is a first-generation Mexican-American. I ask him what he thinks about Donald Trump's braying that the country is being overrun by Mexicans who are drug dealers and rapists. He says quietly that most are good people, but some are not.

Turning into the condo parking lot, we are relieved that the day's trials are behind us. The feeling doesn't last long; our only door key is on the ring I had put into the drop box at Motormania. Uriel and Sophia wait while we sort things out.

I had left a spare key with my son, Murph, but he's out of town. I reach him by phone and learn that the key on his desk at the bakery/restaurant he owns. Uriel takes me to get it, then at 10:00 or so, he and Sophia start the long drive to their home out past Motormania.

I fall asleep with my ambivalence about life in Texas tipped in favor of the positive and with my faith quickened.

CHAPTER THREE
ONCE UPON A TIME

The first explicit indication of the van trip appears in my diary two years before we lock the door of the Austin condo and drive west. But vague hints had danced around much earlier while sitting on the porch of the former Carmelite monastery where we lived. If my diary extended back far enough, foreshadowing would have appeared in my teens. And its basis was formed in childhood. Maybe I was born with it. I think that's how it was with Ann, too.

* * * *

During World War II, my pipefitter father got defense work at an oil refinery in Persia (present-day Iran). I could barely see over the side of the steamer trunk he was filling with work boots and khakis and everything else he would need for the year he would be gone. Or maybe it was eighteen months. I'm not sure. Much of the time before leaving, he was a little sick from inoculations, especially in his telling the one for yellow fever. I don't recall the goodbye moment.

My mother, my brother Bob, and I moved a thousand miles to live with my maternal grandparents in Muskogee.

Mother got one of the two existing bedrooms. Bob and I sort of camped in a small room with a shed roof that they had slapped together for us off the kitchen. It felt like a boys' lean-to clubhouse. I was five. He was ten,

The double bed we shared was up against a kitchen window that had opened to the outdoors before the bedroom was built. Wonder Bread was kept on a table just inside the window, and Bob could reach it without getting up. He did that so often the dentist blamed it for a run of cavities he was having.

I didn't have Bob's bread lust, but young as I was, I loved coffee. For me, the smell of coffee brewing was a surpassing pleasure. When I got old enough to think about what preachers mean by "the peace that passeth all understanding," it occurred to me that it might be something like what I felt when that aroma drifted over our bed, and outside the screen door along the length of the yard next to the hog wire fence were tomatoes, okra, melons, squash, turnips, bell peppers, radishes, carrots, and collard greens, and nightcrawlers made slimy trails across the dew-covered grass, and blue jays screamed wake-up calls like roosters.

My Grandfather (Big Daddy) was a butcher. My Grandmother (Pell – a child's version of Pearl) was a clerk in the town department store. Pell's parents, Pappy and Big Mama, lived about twenty miles south near Warner. They had chickens and guinea fowls, a cow or two, a garden, an outhouse, a storm cellar, and a well. The only running water in the house came out of a hand pump in the kitchen sink.

Big Daddy's parents, Grampaw Jim and Gramaw Molly, lived in a good-sized, two-story house in Webber's Falls, which was nine miles east of Warner. She took in boarders, I think, but I'm a little fuzzy on that. When young, he operated a ferry on the Arkansas River. In my time, he mostly sat on the porch, which was explained later by "he drank, you know," spoken with eyes downcast in a look of sad disapproval. His drinking may have been exaggerated; he died in 1944 at the age of eighty-four. He was said to be a good fiddler, but I never heard him play. My mother played violin in various orchestras until she was around eighty. I suppose there was a connection.

One of Big Daddy's several sisters, Ora, and her husband, Doolin, endured a country life of limited means on a small piece of land somewhere around there. He had a big belly that hung over his belt. Uncle Doolin didn't say much, at least not that I recall. Neither did their son Edwin, my first cousin once removed.

It seems like we were kin to people all over that part of Oklahoma and on into Arkansas. The ones who weren't relatives were friends of long standing.

In an earlier time in more prosperous circumstances when Pappy owned a ranch, he got into a dispute with another rancher about who owned certain cattle. When a lawman (said implausibly in the family telling to be a U.S. Marshall) showed up to reclaim the animals in question, Pappy drew his gun and ran him off. Before the dispute was settled, Big Daddy, Pell's brothers Cliff and Bebb, and Pappy's ranch hands took up arms. The Porum Range War, as it was called, lasted for several years, but the most intense fighting ended after a few days when a train carrying a detachment of special deputies arrived from Muskogee, the county seat. Several people were killed, including nineteen-year-old Cliff. A number more were injured. But Pappy got his cows back. Or so the story went.

Sometimes Big Daddy took off his bloody butcher's apron and delivered groceries in a pickup truck. I rode along with him now and then. He would hunch over the wheel and whistle tunelessly through his teeth, pausing occasionally to roll a cigarette. He claimed he could roll one in the wind on horseback. He showed me how, but I never got the hang of it. He called me "Outfit." I liked that. Ranches were called outfits. If I was an outfit, I was part of Big Daddy's world of cattle, cowboys, and Indians, which by then was already something that existed mostly in movies.

Pell and Big Daddy had found the money to marry when he won a good deal of money in the calf-roping event at a big rodeo. Once at a county fair rodeo, he took me behind the chutes from which calves, bucking horses, and bulls were shunted into the arena. He introduced me to a couple of dusty competitors who were Indians. One was named T.C., the other Notchy. T.C. put five-year-old me on his horse while the men talked. Sometimes, Big Daddy let me hold the six-shooter which he brought with him when he and Pell moved off a ranch where he was foreman into the tiny town of Porum so my mother and her brother could go to school.

In my memory, it was always hot in Muskogee, and Pell was always about to be late for work. Every morning, she scurried around half-dressed, bosom bouncing, in a cloud of bath powder seeking an accommodation between sweat and her girdle and braiding her long hair.

She probably would not have been in such a stew, if she had not dawdled at the breakfast table listening to *The Breakfast Club* and blessing me with a little "coffee milk." "Not, too much," she would caution. "It'll make your feet black on the bottom."

Now and then for the rest of my life, in a rite of remembrance like on All Saints Day, I make a cup of one part coffee, three parts milk, three sugars, and I smell the Tussy. If I were to do the whole ceremony, I would boil the coffee in a tin pot. That's how Big Daddy made it. I don't recall him timing it; he just knew when it was done. Poured carefully, the grounds stayed mostly in the pot. Years later, my brother tried it once when we were camping. He put eggshells in the pot to make the grounds stay put. I don't recall if it worked. Myself, I'm content to have only the memory of that method, though I may show my grandchildren how to do it one of these days if I can get them interested. It would give me a chance to tell them about my enchanted life in Muskogee.

When Daddy arrived home from Persia late one night, Bob and I were sleeping. He piled into our bed and crushed us in an unrestrained embrace. The joy of that moment has not been diminished by time.

Until fairly recently, American men made do with shaking hands to express affection. The only other time I recall embracing Daddy came twenty years later when he was dying. I had been away for an extended period, and he waited, not knowing whether I would get there in time. He was in a wheelchair in a hospital solarium when I arrived. He held out his wasting, once strong working man's arms with the same lack of inhibition he had showed that night in Muskogee. On both occasions we held each other a long time, and on both occasions a life was over.

We left Muskogee for Toledo where Daddy had work in another refinery.

Ann's childhood was as charmed as mine, and hers, too, ended abruptly.

For both of us, joyful early years are as much a part of who we are now as the color of our eyes. Eventually, we would realize the moral shortcomings of that time and place. Learning to live with both views at once would be a life-long undertaking.

CHAPTER FOUR
ON OUR WAY

By my measure, the decrepit Carmelite monastery had about twelve-thousand square feet. Nobody needs a house that big. We sure didn't. But need had nothing to do with it. We walked through twice, then offered full price. We were compelled.

We closed on the purchase on the last day of 1998, and for the next nineteen years, we poured energy and money into renovation. For much of that time, we drove the three hundred miles from our apartment in New York City on Friday evening, worked all weekend painting, tearing down walls, refinishing floors, and trying not to be discouraged by seemingly endless plumbing leaks and boiler malfunctions and electrical problems, and got back to New York City late Sunday evening.

We found pleasure beyond telling in the project, and the house became a fundamental part of our identity. As we settled into the Adirondacks village where it was located, we were welcomed over and over with, "Oh you're the people who bought the Carmelite house." Often that was followed by something like, "Thank you for saving it."

In time, financial reverses forced us to sell the city apartment and make the monastery our sole residence. Then after a bit, we could no longer afford to keep it either. It was hard to sell, though; there was little demand for such a property. Still, it was time to move on to another life.

We tried to find a way to afford living in New York City again. We had felt more at home there than any place we'd ever lived as adults. While worrying about whether we would go broke paying the fuel oil bill and keeping the place in good repair, we read real estate ads and thought about how small an apartment we could live in.

From time to time, we tried on another possibility. "How about moving back to Austin? Cost of living is less than New York. (As it turned out, the difference was less than we thought.) We have old friends there. Family." We couldn't warm to the idea, though. Austin didn't have Lincoln Center or the Metropolitan Museum or an Anglo-Catholic church.

Out of this stew of disquiet came an outside-the-box idea. Maybe a campervan was the answer to who to be and how to live. Sell the monastery for whatever we could get. Hit the road. Have no fixed address for an indefinite period. But that didn't quite fill the need either. Finding peace through driving around in a van for a long time didn't have the dignity or sophistication or grandness that salvation, even the temporal kind, should come wrapped in. Still, a small taste of van life sounded like fun, and we really needed to have some of that. So, a couple of months later, we rented a camper and explored Yosemite and environs. It didn't begin to fill the hole, though. For my part, it was not even much fun.

When it was over, I wrote the following in my diary.

I won't make a campervan trip again. The campgrounds were rough and dirty. Slogging to the distant privy in the cold and rain was unpleasant, and my aged prostate required several trips a night. We enjoyed some dry sunny weather, but not enough. That last night at an RV site close to the Pacific in Half Moon Bay was especially chilly, wet, and dirty. Got lost in rush-hour traffic trying to find it. Up at 4:00 the next morning to avoid traffic getting to the van-rental place. Driving in fog over to Highway 101 was harrowing.

About two years after writing those words, a truck pulled up in front of the house in Austin where we had settled despite reservations and unloaded a 1971 Volkswagen Westfalia camper we had bought online.

I had reasons to believe that this van adventure in the making would be much more to my liking than the earlier one. Actually, I expected it to be just about perfect: a break from ordinary life, a learning experience, and an overdue improvement in mental health. (I'll get back to the last point down the page.) An exciting new life awaited.

My thinking went something like this.

A VW Westie has a delightful *je ne sais quoi* we did not find in the converted Ford panel truck we rented in California.

We'll climb in and put on a happy face. Ann will become the flower child she once was; I, as free a spirit as a man my age can be; Baby Kitty will jump up on the dashboard and look like a *Family Circle* cover.

We'll spread sunshine all over the place. At our passing, people of a certain age will flash peace signs and slip back into the age of Aquarius. Classic-car enthusiasts will swoon even if they've never heard of Woodstock; the van has its original "Chianti-red" paint, it's rust-free, it's in showroom condition.

It'll be like walking a Labrador puppy. We'll be surrounded by admiring throngs at campgrounds from Caprock Canyons to Lopez Island. It will be ever so much more to our liking than arriving in that converted Ford panel truck.

The trip would have occasional problems, of course. For one thing, it's certain we'll get lost now and then. We are really good at getting lost. Never mind. We were going to rely entirely on paper maps; a GPS would violate the spirit of the adventure. We would respond to getting lost and to all untoward incidents by declaiming in chorus some words of G. K. Chesterton we'll have pasted on the dashboard. "An inconvenience is only an adventure wrongly considered; an adventure is only an inconvenience rightly considered."

To that point in our lives, such composure had been elusive. We were good at being impatient and anxious, but detachment had appeared only rarely. We figured if we could manage to believe Chesterton's dictum wholeheartedly when facing off against grizzlies and heavily armed White nationalists in northern Idaho or other such trials, we might be able to do so in ordinary circumstances after we got back home, and the trip would have afforded more than mere pleasure. This is what I meant when I mentioned mental-health improvement above.

CHAPTER FIVE
A TONKA TOY WITH A GROWL

When shopping for a van, the ads on the computer screen offered little other than excitement. I had owned a VW van in the early seventies, but I knew nothing about it except that it was the cool car of the time. The only work I ever did on it was to take out the rear seat, put in a playpen for my younger sons, and add a couple of director's chairs. It came with seat belts, but like most people at the time, we didn't use them. Regular maintenance was handled by the dealer where I'd bought it, and it never even had a flat tire.

We needed expert advice. A company named Motormania advertised over thirty years' experience working on VWs, old and new, and invited customers to "call for a free consultation." That was for me. Phoning wouldn't do, though; I had a laptop full of descriptions I wanted experts to look at. I drove to the shop on the outskirts of Austin for in-person counsel.

In many ways, its office is like many independent-garage offices – grimy and short on space and attended by a big scary dog, in this case an Alsatian named Tango. He barks menacingly when I enter but stops when Roger, one of the two brothers who own the shop, gently shushes him. Two worn chairs face a counter behind which Roger answers the phone, takes deliveries of parts, talks now and them with one of the mechanics, and does business with customers. Old rock music I can't identify plays in the background.

Somehow, Roger makes me feel like I have his full attention. And he is genuinely interested in what I've come to see him about. Like a good primary-care doctor. Or a new old friend.

Over the next few months, we talk about all kinds of things: his studying to be a geologist before the love of old VWs took over his life, treatments for enlarged prostates, and the cruel grief that follows the loss of a pet. He had to wait several years before getting Tango; couldn't face the pain of loss again. He had recently spent a thousand dollars to get Tango's heart trouble treated. "I *had* to," he said. Ann and I spend freely, one might say extravagantly, on Baby Kitty, so I get it, even though I don't find Alsatians to be pet-like. Maybe I've seen too many World War II movies. And as a child, I saw one eat a kitten.

Tango belies the stereotype. He sits down next to me, and once I get my nerve up, he welcomes my petting. He's as agreeable as a lap dog unless I try to pet Roger's other dog, a Shih Tzu named Duke.

"Tango gets jealous if you pay attention to Duke."

I don't know if Roger's brother, Tom, has a dog. He and his wife do have six cats. Used to have twelve.

Soon after I get to know him, Tom recites Motormania's founding myth. I'm guessing it's much the same at old-VW garages all around the country.

"When Rog was sixteen, he bought a '69 Beetle. One day our dad came home and found that Rog had taken it apart while trying to fix something. Pieces were all over the garage floor. Dad shook his head and said he would never get it put back together. That was all it took. Some years later, I bought it from Rog." He points to the rack behind him. "That's it."

I give it a superficial once-over and express admiration, but as quickly as courtesy permits, I open my computer and show them a beautifully restored 1967 camper known as a "splitty" for its two-pane windshield. It has an excellent new pale-blue paint job. It's movie-star photogenic. But when I explain that I plan to drive it to Washington state and spend a few months on the road, they give each other the side eye, then talk me out of it. I may have confessed right off that knowing how to shift gears is about the limit of my knowledge of auto mechanics. Or maybe they could tell just by looking at me; they'd been in the business a long time. Anyway, they know.

They point out that this classic would impress the VW buffs at car shows, but it wouldn't be much of a road car. A highly skilled hobbyist whose fingernails were seldom free of grease and who had plenty of money would enjoy owning it. I don't qualify. It's good advice, and it's selfless. The thing would be in their shop so often, Ann and I would be funding a substantial portion of their retirement.

For several months I show them ads, until persuaded by nothing more than words and photos, a passing grade on a prepurchase inspection, and no spoil-sport caveats from Tom and Roger, we write a big check to a classic-car dealer in Chicago. A few weeks later, it emerges from a covered transport truck, gleaming like a new Tonka toy, its powerful replacement engine growling like the MGM lion, and bearing promise of adventure.

It's well preserved, and it has been restored and updated in various ways, but it needs more. Of course, it does; it's forty-seven years old.

CHAPTER SIX
TRIAL RUNS

One day in spring, as a trial run, we drive the van ninety miles to spend a weekend with friends at their ranch. It runs a little hot, so I take it to Tom and Roger to see if they can do anything about it before summer arrives. They install an oil cooler and make some other changes, and I drive away confident that the tendency of air-cooled engines to overheat will not be a problem for us, not even in Texas.

But just to be sure, after the weather gets hot, we make a longer trial run to the little town of Rockport on the Texas coast for a week of fishing with old friends. We'd been doing that almost every summer for decades, coming from as far away as New York and London. It's reassuring and restorative like the major Feast Days in the liturgical calendar.

Even right after Hurricane Harvey has had its way with the town and with rebuilding only beginning, being there is still mostly about fishing, watching the sun rise and set over the Gulf of Mexico, keeping an eye out for flights of roseate spoonbills, and the sweet comfort of being with old friends.

Hurricane damage is everywhere; the town has taken a direct hit. In a way, though, it feels the same as always.

Some years earlier, when I still had hair, I said to a barber that it was wonderful the way Rockport hardly ever changed. He, a year-round resident and, as it turned out, quite the civic booster, took offense. I left the shop looking like Kim Jong Un would years later.

Our disagreement had little to do with facts. He could have showed me strip centers being constructed and expensive new houses. I could have told him that I was staying in the same assemblage of

1920s tourist cabins where I had been staying for years, but that would have been beside the point. For me, absence of change was about the ineffable and immeasurable, about how it *feels* in Rockport.

As we often have, Walle (pronounced "Wally") and Shaaron (pronounced "Sharon"), Joe and Carolyn, and Ann and I stay in "the "big house" that had been the residence of the manager/owner of the tourist cabins.

A few years before the trial-run, it burned to the ground. The owners rebuilt the exterior exactly as it had been before, but inside, they added another bathroom and air conditioning and generally tarted it up. I have mixed feelings about these improvements. We had a lot of happy times there when pots and pans were hung on twelve-penny nails, the floor at the back sloped off precipitously, beds were pushed close to the windows to catch the breeze off the water, we waited in line for the bathroom, and we sweated. Boy did we sweat. But even with the changes, to me it still seems pretty much the same.

We used to pile into Walle's boat before daylight and bounce full throttle toward the barrier island two or three miles across the bay. In a nod to proper running lights, someone in the bow would hold up a flashlight. After a time, we'd anchor, jump out into shallow water, and spend the day wading in pursuit of trout and redfish. We wore ordinary sneakers, heavy-when-wet jeans, and we didn't bother with stingray guards. For some reason now lost to history, we would sustain ourselves with no more than a Peanut Plank and water. I suggested once or twice that we take sandwiches and beer, but I couldn't get anyone interested. Peanut Planks and water had been the way since before I started showing up, and no one saw any reason to change. We kept more fish than would be allowed today, and many would be too small by current regulations.

Evenings, we would sit on the porch and watch the bay be the bay and wish that the warm breeze wouldn't melt the ice in our drinks so fast. Then we would gather at a round table under a creaking ceiling fan for ceviche, fried fish, sometimes shrimp and crabs. As years passed, we began to turn in earlier and not stay out all day and some days, we wouldn't fish at all. The van is a frivolous addition to the serious business of fishing and all that went with it. To call the drive to the coast a trial run is a little wide of the mark. We had already made the trial run to the Osborns' ranch and followed up with some precautionary changes. The trip to the coat is more of a victory lap than a test. In any case, its performance is flawless. In other respects, the week suggests challenges to come, though they don't register as such at the time.

In addition to checking the van's mechanical worthiness, we are on the lookout for issues that might arise when we load it with everything we will be taking. We were excited, and we lived near an REI store, so we had bought what seemed like one or two of every item in its inventory except equipment for mountain climbing, artic trekking, and cycling. From a company in England, we ordered a tent the size of a New York apartment. From Home Depot, tools, which neither of us were any good at using, plus flares, reflective vests, and bungy cords. We pack clothes suitable for situations other than camping, such as maybe the Santa Fe opera or a church service. And BK's litter box and kitty backpack with screened sides so she wouldn't have to stay in the van when we went hiking, a big box of Lactated Ringers drip bags to treat her failing kidneys, and a silly amount of pet paraphernalia. If the van won't hold everything on the Rockport trip, we'll have time to decide what to leave behind when we take the drive out west.

Also, we intend to practice stowing each item according to frequency of use and ease of accessibility. The spare tire will be buried since we don't want to mount it over the front bumper or on the roof, but things like flashlights and band aids need to be easy to get at. And after carefully arriving at best order, there will still be the challenge of remembering where exactly we put them. I consider making a diagram:

camp stove and cooking utensils right rear compartment, hiking boots under the back seat, and so on. But that doesn't seem in keeping with playing like summer-of-love free spirits for a while.

The Rockport trip doesn't help much with these issues, It can't. We still don't have "everything."

Anyway, we run out of time and have to shove in what we do have creating something like a teenager's bedroom. Nor do we use the rooftop luggage carrier that we will stuff and secure with bungy cords on the trip out west; I've not yet bought a ladder.

The fishing doesn't go as planned either; actually, for me, it doesn't go at all. On the drive down, a minor rash changes from a job for Cortisone to something that suggests I should ring a bell and wear a sign saying "unclean."

Advanced as it is, modern medicine can offer neither cure nor symptomatic relief. This is disappointing, as the itching is extreme. After a couple of rough nights, I start numbing the affected areas, which is just about everything but my feet and face, by piling on ice packs kind of like we do with fish out in the boat.

An allergic reaction to a drug, they say. Stay out of the sun and don't get overheated, they say. Bathe in oatmeal. Looks like you'll just have to tough it out. A drug that is supposed to counteract the drug reaction that is tormenting me turns out to have unpleasant side effects of its own. A medium-strong prescription for back pain helps some, but not as much as I want. I've left the heavy artillery in Austin, or I would chug a jumbo dose.

Another objective of the coast trip is to practice pitching the big English tent, which was said to be a simple undertaking. I watch the manufacturer's how-to video several times, but after every viewing, I consider sending the thing back across the Atlantic and getting a refund of the many hundred dollars we paid for it.

It's designed to attach to the side of the van where the sliding door is. Properly set up, it functions as a spare room that can be entered without getting rained on. It's possible to detach the tent without taking the whole thing down when you have to drive away for beer and other necessities. Trouble is, upon returning – beer waiting to be opened – you have to park the van exactly – to the millimeter – where it had been before thirst struck. It's a tedious two-person job that makes use of little cones that you place by the wheels before driving away.

It would have been much simpler and way less expensive to use an ordinary tent, set it up near – not flush against – the van and accept having to take a step or two through open air to enter it. That wouldn't be exactly Lewis-and-Clark-level hardship. Nothing doing, though. No sir. When properly attached, the nifty English tent will keep BK from wandering off into the forest to be eaten by bears. We deny her nothing.

None of this matters, though. Repeatedly erecting it, taking it down, and stowing the thing in July in Texas until we got the hang of it is unappealing as a vacation activity. Actually, it's impossible, if you are under medical directions to stay out of the sun and not get overheated. Never mind. We'll come to grips with tent assembly somewhere on a cool mountainside in New Mexico.

After a week in Rockport, we run up the white flag and start for Austin to see my dermatologist. Before leaving, we do make one valuable bit of trip preparation. It's forced on us when we lock the keys inside the van. Getting into a locked car was easy before cars got so sophisticated, but none of the ways we used then work on the van. Not hooking the lock button with a twisted clothes hanger. Not poking that flat tool thing down beside the window into the innards of the door where the locking mechanism is. Nothing works except picking the lock the way private eyes and crooks do in movies. Fortunately, there is a guy in Rockport who can do that. We make a second set of keys, and Ann wears them as a charm on her bracelet for the duration of the trip.

So, though we tried, we will start the adventure without being fully prepared. We have not even decided on a return date. That, at least, is not a problem; after about eight weeks on the road, we will realize vaguely that we are finding what we had not known we were looking for and we can start back toward Austin and when we get there, be the people we had become.

CHAPTER SEVEN
OFF AGAIN, ON AGAIN

Two days before we start for Lopez Island, I take the van to Tom and Roger for a final checkup. I arrive as soon as they open and plan to be there only an hour or two. I don't get away until midafternoon. They are determined to be sure both van and I are ready for the challenges of the road.

They install a new battery. They warn me that if the oil light comes on, I should stop *immediately*; driving just a little farther to that gas station up ahead will burn up the engine. Tom gives me some hard-to-find fuses to keep in the glove compartment, and he shows me how to install them. He puts extra air in the tires to accommodate the load we'll be carrying. He sells me a V belt. Like fuses, they won't be readily available on the road, but he warns that putting one on will be complicated by the mechanism of the air conditioning system we have added; we will need a good mechanic. The warning is unnecessary; I don't know a V belt from a timing chain.

They teach me a lot. Or at least they try to. When school lets out, I can talk oil temperature and fuses and such, but it's like reciting something in a foreign language that I don't speak; I make the sounds without knowing much at all about what they mean. Still, I appreciate their efforts. They know that old VWs break down, and they do everything they can to keep that from happening. But if it does, they want me to have parts and a plan for dealing with it.

To them, fixing old VWs is not a job; it's a vocation. Roger jokes that, worst case, he'll throw tools into his old Cessna and fly to wherever I am. I think he might.

Finally, hearty abrazos, and a mechanic's blessing: "safe travels and no breakdowns."

I leave the garage feeling optimistic and eager and sure that the van is ready. I plan to start loading as soon as I get home. I don't make it home, though. Well, *I* do, but the van doesn't. In heavy traffic in central Austin, it stops running.

I turn the key over and over and sweat and hold up traffic and try to figure out what to do. Before I get anywhere near forming a plan, a man in a pickup truck stops to help.

Over the honking, he shouts, "You got a chain?"

A chain? I'm carrying a lot of stuff for emergencies, but not a chain. I guess the guy thought the van was so likely to break down, any sensible person would be carrying one.

He phones a friend to bring one, waves traffic around me until the friend arrives, then lies down on the blistering hot pavement, reaches under the van, connects the chain, and maneuvers truck and van through a turnstile into a nearby parking lot.

His name is Joe Rodriguez. He's a cheerful man, covered in construction-work dust and sweat. I try to give him some money – not a "tip," but more what the church calls a thank offering. He won't take it.

"I have a grandfather," he says. Then he goes back to his job pouring concrete.

By the time a wrecker shows up more than two hours later, gratefulness to Joe Rodriguez is giving way to negative thoughts about the van adventure. Not just the trip either; something more along the line of what the hell did we think we were doing buying a vehicle that is likely to destroy so much stomach lining.

I have a low tolerance for frustration. When my computer acts up, I give serious consideration to becoming a total Luddite. My old friend Peggy doesn't have a computer, and though she has a cell phone, I don't think it's a smart phone, and anyway she doesn't answer it, she only calls out on it, and she gets along just fine that way. The lesson of her behavior is clear and simple: if something, such as computers – or a classic VW – frustrates you a lot, get rid of it.

The wrecker is driven by a proud Marine Corps veteran named Jimmy. His truck is not air-conditioned, and his garage is thirty miles down Interstate 35, which, as usual, is jammed with NAFTA-generated trucks. He's dripping sweat. Unlike me, he's calm and upbeat.

"Why did AAA call *you*? There are wreckers available in Austin."

"Because they know I will come," he says. I guess wrecker drivers tend to be unreliable. I don't pursue it.

We talk about what it's like driving a tow truck for a living. He says he's been doing it for years, and helping people in trouble squares with his Christian values. While he pulls the van up onto the back of the wrecker and makes it secure, he offers words of encouragement. As he's leaving, he assures me that "when you think the loving God has gone to sleep, He hasn't. He's always there, ready to help." I've been a committed Christian my whole life, but in-your-face, born-again witnessing makes me uncomfortable. When someone starts in with it, I suddenly find I'm late for an appointment.

In the summer before first grade, my Presbyterian family sent me to Vacation Bible School at First Baptist Church in Muskogee. My mother must have been desperate to get me out of the house; my people were contemptuous of Baptists. Only Catholics were more disdained.

At the end of the term, a preacher issued an altar call to the assembled children. He implored us to come to the front of the church and give ourselves to Jesus. I was a compliant child, eager to please, and so I did. One evening a couple of weeks later, I was summoned in from the yard where I was catching fireflies to explain to my mother and grandparents (who were laughing) and to a man I didn't know, why I wanted to join First Baptist. I had no idea that's what giving my soul to Jesus had meant.

In high school, I attended Morning Watch, a daily student-led worship service held in the auditorium for a half hour or so before the bell rang. I liked the gospel songs and hymns. Still do. They were as much fun as any other kind of singing. But the testifying and windy praying became increasingly distasteful, a view I've held ever since.

Standing there by the wrecker wiping my brow, altar calls and the Jesus talk of evangelicals have long since been replaced by sacramental faith. Still, I rather welcome Jimmy's witnessing.

Like Joe, Jimmy won't accept a thank offering.

When I get to Motormania the next morning, Tom reports that the van started right up. High temperature had caused the fuel to vaporize. He wraps the fuel line with insulation and cautions me to drive slowly enough so that the needle on the oil temperature gauge doesn't go past its midpoint, which is around 220 degrees.

For the second time in two days, I leave Motormania encouraged and enthusiastic about the trip. It's a long way from what I felt while sweating out the breakdown the afternoon before. Is owning the van making me bipolar?

I spend the rest of the day excitedly tending to last-minute items – return a library book, buy a pair of driving gloves and a D battery for a lamp, get cash, and take a key to our condo to my son Murph. Ann and I eat all the perishables we can hold and throw away the remainder.

This thing is going to happen after all.

CHAPTER EIGHT
GIFTS

On a Christmas Eve years earlier, snow was falling on the former monastery with near whiteout force. We had set a table in front of an open fire in an attempt at a festive dinner. Pain and fear would not allow it.

A few days earlier, without warning and for no good reason, Ann had been fired (in the more telling British phrase, "made redundant") from her position as a Managing Director at a global financial services firm. She'd had little experience with failure – none with any so serious as this – and she was staggered by it.

At the time, she was in transition to a role more to her liking, one with less stress overall, a corner office, and fewer all-night transatlantic flights that spit her out into conference rooms where she was often the only woman.

"It's not personal," they said. "The firm is downsizing."

She is left to guess why she is at the top of the list of those being let go.

The consequences would extend far beyond a bruised ego and being temporarily out of a job.

She was a fifty-five-year-old, highly specialized, expensive attorney who was severely handicapped in the international banking world by lack of a penis. It would be difficult to find another position.

Early in our marriage, we had agreed that she would embrace the opportunities that came her way as an outstanding student at a highly regarded law school. They included living in New York, London, Hong Kong, and Zurich. I happily became a corporate wife, aka trailing spouse, and turned to pursuit of the writing vocation I had been more or less defined by since college. As a consequence, my earnings were limited to the small rewards of free-lance writing and part-time teaching. Despite Ann's hours often being way too long and the day-to-day pressure great, it was an agreeable way to live.

She was paid handsomely, and we had a financial plan that would have worked well, but for her dismissal. At the time of the miserable Christmas Eve dinner, we owned a small apartment in New York City and the former monastery, but we had little cash. We were, however, nearing the end of the barely tolerable renovation expenses and were about to start funding retirement. As we picked at our food, it seemed likely that enjoying the rest of our lives in the historic home we had restored was not to be. In addition, we sensed that financial stress would be but part of the pain.

We talk little, and hardly taste the food. The wound is fresh; we have not begun to come to terms with it.

Baby Kitty hears it first. On her cushion near the fire, she rises up on her hind legs like a prairie dog and jerks her head around to stare at the front windows. From the darkness comes the sound of young voices singing the eternal promise of the season: "Silent night, holy night. All is calm, all is bright." We sit without moving or speaking, taking in the mystery of the words and the moment. When the singing ends, we rush to the door, and turn on the porch light.

A woman and three children are disappearing into falling snow. "Merry Christmas," we shout. "Come in and have something to drink."

But they are gone.

We stare into the darkness until cold drives us back inside. It's the only time anyone has ever come to us singing carols.

Over the next two-and-a-half years, Ann has numerous interviews, all of them positions she is well qualified for. Each rejection destroys a piece of who she is, and the chipping away accumulates.

We put the monastery on the market, but even at a price well below what we have invested in it, no one is interested. We sell the city apartment, begin living on the proceeds, and make the monastery our sole residence. We can keep up with operating expenses for a time, but it's a financial drain, and we can't continue it indefinitely.

On another windy, frigid evening with snow swirling and cold air leaking into the old house at numerous points, we huddle by the stove in my second-floor study, and as we've been doing frequently, we go over possibilities. We come up with nothing of promise and are sinking into hopelessness, when the doorbell rings.

It's late, and we're in no mode for visitors, so I ignore it. But on the third ring, I drag myself down to see who is there. From the top of the stairs, I make out the back of someone in a broad-brimmed, black hat and a long cloak-like outer garment.

When I turn on the porch light, the figure turns to face me. I'm startled. It's our old friend, Father Dan, a Franciscan priest who used to live across the street. But now he lives in Toronto. He hasn't been in town since he left a year or two ago. I didn't know he was here.

"Dan?"

He smiles and says nothing, and we embrace, and he, who drinks little, pulls a bottle of single-malt Scotch from under his coat. We go upstairs and join Ann. I put more wood on the fire. For a couple of hours, we drink whisky and talk. We tell him about our situation and confess our faithless fears and worldly anxieties. He listens. No clerical platitudes. No dogma. No, "you shouldn't feel that way." No advice. When it's time for him to go, he puts his hands on our heads and blesses us in the ancient way, and we weep. Like the carolers, he disappears into the snow, leaving us renewed and strengthened.

After another few months, Ann abandons her search for a legal position. It has led to nothing but disappointment and defeat. And because of her specialization and other factors, it's all but impossible for her to make a go of opening her own office. She has to accept that she will never again practice law. She has not lost her job; she has been stripped of her license, like a priest being defrocked.

Reluctantly, she begins taking steps to start a baking business. In the basement, the monastery has a second kitchen with a commercial mixer and extra sinks. I have experience in opening and running a bakery. She is an accomplished commercial baker. But she enrolled in law school at age thirty to get away from baking for a living. At every moment, the return to baking says to her that she has failed as a lawyer.

In the midst of this dispiriting attempt, she gets a phone call that is as mysterious and life giving as the visit from the carolers and Father Dan – an unsolicited offer of an attorney position. It pays far less than she made at her peak, but other aspects of it make up for that. It will involve legal work of a type and a level of complexity she had mastered years earlier. She will work at home or wherever she happens to be via internet and telephone. It will be part time at first but probably with more hours in the future. She says "Yes" immediately and keeps saying "Yes" until the caller runs out of questions. Only Molly Bloom said "yes" with such fervor.

By the time we set off for Lopez Island, we have come to realize that losing her high-powered job was providential. The work was emotionally destructive, and, near the end, it was beginning to affect her health, but in something like the Stockholm syndrome, walking away from it of her own volition always seemed too disruptive.

CHAPTER NINE
NOW WHAT?

I like Sundays to be the way they were during the Muskogee years. They would begin with a special breakfast, usually including biscuits, sometimes pork chops. Big Daddy would spoon sorghum molasses on his biscuits. I think he was the only one who ate sorghum. I tried it once, but as much as I wanted to be like him, I thought it was awful. The last thing before leaving for church, he would push his sugar intake to a celestial level by having a toddy, his one drink of the week. He'd be asleep before the preacher got warmed up.

These elements were constant, but there were a couple of variables in addition. Sometimes a young soldier from nearby Camp Gruber would be at the table after spending the night on a pallet in the living room. And some Sundays, it would be Pell's turn to take the church flowers to the VA hospital and distribute them among the patients.

The biggest meal of the week was after church – usually chuck roast with potatoes and carrots. Then the adults would take a nap, and Bob and I would be directed to "find something to do," and not disturb them. After a light supper, we would listen to Jack Benny, *Fibber McGee and Molly*, and other shows on the radio.

Ann recalls the Sundays of her childhood being much the same as mine, though she's almost a generation younger.

It was a time of stillness and certainty.

This Sunday after the roadside encounter with the angel Cindy is nothing like that. We wake feeling anxious and burdened with "now what are we going to do?" The sense of being taken care of, which had fended off worry at bedtime, hadn't lasted through the night.

Coffee would help, but it's in the van. We go to a café for breakfast, something I wouldn't normally do. The first hour or so of any day, especially Sunday, is a time to be alone, drinking coffee, wool-gathering, getting my game face on.

Back at the condo after breakfast, I turn to reading about fuel vaporization. I already know enough about it to be pretty sure it was what had stopped us. Driving an air-cooled German vehicle in summer in Texas is asking for it.

I find a number of possibilities for preventing vapor lock. None offer much promise. One recommendation is to use a fuel additive designed to make gasoline less volatile, but it doesn't get high marks from reviewers. It seems to work no better than a trick Ann and I had used when we lived in the Adirondacks. We would add kerosene to the heating oil, which would give it a better chance of making it from the storage tank under the driveway to the boiler in the basement without freezing. It was an effective ploy except when it was needed most – when temperatures were extremely cold. The only way to be certain that the fuel didn't freeze was to move the storage tanks into the warm basement. I am looking for an equally effective defense against vapor lock.

Another suggestion is to use ethanol-free gasoline. It's more stable than gas that contains ethanol. With a just a few keystrokes I call up a nationwide directory of stations where it's sold, including one in Austin. I drive over in our Prius to check. They don't sell it, and they have no idea why they are listed in the directory.

A little more research reveals that ethanol-free gasoline is more likely to be found in cooler parts of the country, not where we will need it most. Besides that, many of the places that sell it are marinas, where the pumps are on boat docks. A picture forms in my mind of filling jerry cans and lugging them to the van that would be far away in a parking lot. And I recall that the marina near the former monastery would sell only to boats.

I ask my great-nephew Maitland for advice. By day, he's an engineer, but he's passionate about small vehicles with small engines. He can fix anything, except, as it turns out, my vapor-lock problem. He suggests that I spray ice water on the fuel line and carburetor. Well, sure – if you happen to have ice water and a spritzer handy and you can get to parts of the engine where the vaporized fuel is lurking. And anyway, I'm looking for a way to *prevent* vaporization, not a fix to apply after it has already ruined my day.

I turn to cancelling campground and motel reservations. In an effort to promote marital harmony, I had gone along with Ann's need to know with certainty where we would spend our nights. Smiling front-desk people at state parks and La Quintas are eagerly awaiting our arrival at stops far into the future.

Ann and I have different ideas about what is the most enjoyable way to make a road trip.

I like to fool around, meander, take side roads, follow impulses, and stop wherever we happen to be when the sun goes down or it's time to have a drink, whichever comes first. Ann prefers having a plan and reservations.

When we do it my way, we risk winding up in one of those motels that attaches price tags on all items not securely attached to floors or walls so you'll know how much you'll be billed if you can't resist stealing a threadbare towel or an aged TV. Rows of idling tractor-trailer rigs rumble just outside the window, and the "free breakfast" consists of small donut-shaped objects that can easily be confused with machine parts and coffee so weak you can see the bottom of the paper cup. Over the years, Ann has become unwilling to risk such nights.

Anyway, we plan to camp most nights, and camping does require reservations. Campgrounds are crowded in August, and only a limited number have power hookups and internet connections necessary for Ann to keep up with her law practice.

So, when the van broke down, we had a number of reservations lined up.

On Sunday afternoon, I start down the list. I had cancelled the Clovis reservation while waiting for Billy Murphy and his truck. Next up is the campground at Ute Lake State Park in New Mexico. Then a motel in Santa Fe where we planned to visit with old friends. At a week out, I stop, holding onto the possibility of quickly getting the van running properly and by eliminating a few stops, catching up with the planned itinerary somewhere in northern Colorado or Wyoming.

If that is not to be, if the van is going to require a radical overhaul, we might make a radical adjustment and scrap the trip entirely. Just park the mobile money pit, maybe sell it, and have a nice long trip in the Prius without doing much camping. Maybe none. Or we could skip the en-route sightseeing, fly to Seattle, rent a car, drive around the Northwest some, enjoy the ten days on Lopez Island where we have rented a house, and while we are there, consider the possibility that we may not be old-VW-van people.

But even as we think surrender, we never stray far from the original vision of driving all over the west in the official vehicle of the Age of Aquarius and having fun. We've spent more than a year improving the van's roadworthiness. It would be hard to accept not continuing. But so far, we aren't getting what we expected. There is a good chance that Chesterton himself would be thinking of throwing in the towel. We go to sleep Sunday night feeling pretty used up.

CHAPTER TEN
A CRUCIAL QUESTION

Tom phones first thing in the morning to say the van had started right up, just like it had after the breakdown a week earlier. Overnight, the vaporized fuel had turned back into liquid. He has some ideas about how to eliminate the "guess work." That seems a weak approximation of what we are experiencing, but I don't argue word choice with him.

"Come out and let me show you what I have in mind." His tone gives me new hope. Maybe we'll salvage the trip yet.

On the drive to the garage, my hope wavers. Does he have something in mind that we can depend on? Is the van ever going to be up to hot-weather driving? The one I owned in the early seventies ran without problems on frequent three-hundred-mile trips between where I lived on the Mexican border and Austin, but that was before ethanol came into use. Or maybe I had been lucky. It might not be possible to alter this van enough so that it doesn't get vapor locked. If it is possible, how much more are we willing to spend? Is it time to cut our losses and sell it to some Yankee who can drive it around Duluth or Presque Isle all summer without problems? (And if he does have a problem, it's *his* problem, not mine. Yes.)

Tom is standing out front when we arrive. Normally, he would be under a car. Is he waiting for us?

He and Roger are thoroughly invested in our project. It has been that way from the first time we showed up. For some reason, they like Ann and me, and they are wowed by the vehicle. Tom has warned me to keep it clean and waxed, and if it gets any dings or scratches and I don't make them disappear, he and Roger won't be responsible for what some old-van enthusiast might do to us. They are almost as excited about our trip as we are.

Tom raises the rack the van is on, and we duck under it. He points out the fuel pump, fuel line, carburetor, and other parts. He explains how when gasoline passes through the fuel line in hot weather, the combined outside and engine temperatures will sometimes cause it to vaporize. I know that already, and he knows I do. It seems he's starting at the beginning in the interest of thoroughness. Vapor lock is more likely to occur in stop-and-go driving. He explains why, but I can't get focused on it. I guess I'm not really classic-Westie material; I just want him to fix it. Vapor lock is aggravated by the fuel pump being located on top of the engine, which acts as a hotplate.

Wrapping the line with insulation hasn't helped enough. That's another thing I already know. Nor has driving with the air conditioning turned off. That too. Nor has adding a thermostatically controlled oil-cooler fan; it blows hot air. Even BK could understand that.

The introduction over, he gets to the point. The only thing that can help now is to install an electric fuel pump. I don't know what causes fuel to flow in the existing one, but it isn't electricity. He also recommends adding a looped fuel line. I don't understand how it works, but I know too little to find anything wrong with adding it. And third, he would move the new fuel pump from its place on the top of the hot engine to as close as possible to the carburetor. That sure makes sense.

As he talks, I start guessing at how much this work will cost. Every time we've spent more on an improvement, we've told ourselves that it will raise the resale value, but it can't go up indefinitely. Maybe it's time to stop this investment program and let American Express try to survive without our van improvement charges.

We retreat to a Tex-Mex restaurant down the road to talk about it over tacos. We drive in silence, each forming a position privately. I expect Ann to go negative and say it's time to concede defeat. I'm optimistic by nature, and it would be natural for me to believe that this fuel pump fix will make the thing as reliable as a new BMW, but I, too, am about ready to call it quits.

Ann surprises me. We are sipping beer and thinking while waiting on our tacos (bean and avocado, no cheese), when she says – declaims, actually – with the same finality she said, "let's have some FUN!" just before we committed to buying the van – "let's do it." Well, why not?

Waiting for parts and installation, I rethink our plan to use a canvas carrier on the luggage rack. Since it can't be locked, it will require unloading and reloading anytime we stay at a motel. That's a lot of work; it's jam full. Humping all that stuff up and down the ladder would be good exercise, but my dicey back might not hold up under the strain. So, I shop for a hard carrier that can be locked. It turns out, they are all so long we wouldn't be able to raise the pop-up roof.

It occurs to me, though, that we can ask strangers to help with the loading and unloading. It would be a peculiar person who wouldn't want to get involved with a beautifully restored Westie, and we'd probably meet some nice people.

The work is finished by the end of the week. When I go out to pick it up, Tom recommends that before starting the trip I make a test drive to the town of Fredericksburg in the hill country west of Austin during the hottest part of the day. He's a bright guy, but he hadn't thought that through.

Fredericksburg is seventy-five miles away. If this latest fix fails, I want it to happen close by the garage, preferably in its parking lot. I drive back and forth on the busy highway in front of the garage for two hours – about one mile to the west, then one mile to the east, as fast as traffic permits. Several stoplights, which aggravate the tendency to vapor lock, add to the thoroughness of the test. The first few times I pass the garage, I honk and wave, but then the horn quits working. No overheating and no vapor lock, though. Tom installs a new horn.

The brothers come out to the parking lot to see me off. "Be sure to text us pictures. ...Remember: when the oil light comes on, stop immediately. ...Good luck with your kitty." Hearty abrazos, and I'm off. They are proud, apprehensive parents sending a quasi-adult child off to college or military service.

Before loading the van, Ann and I take it to a car wash. In addition to removing dirt and protecting the well-preserved forty-eight-year-old paint, it's a purification rite like a priest's ablutions before consecrating the elements in the eucharist. At the time, we're not thinking about the trip in such a grandiose way, but we do understand washing the van to be in some way a meaning-investing act – a prelude and a preparation for something more than just a vacation.

At around 5:30, Tom phones.

"I forgot to give you any oil to take with you."

"Well, thanks, Tom, but motor oil is available everywhere, isn't it?"

"Sure. But the kind I'm giving you is better than ordinary 30-weight. It contains zinc. And be sure you check the level every day." I've had enough old-van class for one week, so I don't ask what the point of zinc is. I still don't know, though other mechanics along the way will also recommend it.

Tom will leave two quarts of it for us on a ledge by the second bay of his shop. We can pick them up on our way out of town.

It's touching to be so cared for. And it's another indication that we are doing more than fixing up an interesting old vehicle and taking a long trip in it.

CHAPTER ELEVEN
OFF AND RUNNING

We are up at 4:00 like the week before, but this time, we drink all the water we can hold and stow enough in the van to last through even the longest breakdown on the hottest day on the least-traveled road in bleakest west Texas.

We pick up the two quarts of zinc-containing oil that Tom has left for us, and by 8:30, we are clear of Austin sprawl. A couple of hours later, we skate past the little roadside park where we had broken down. I acknowledge it with a toot of the new horn, and watch it fade from sight in the rear-view mirror.

We arrive in Lubbock 372 miles later feeling victorious and confident. We have gotten through the day without any mechanical problems. The adventure is not yet very interesting, but that will come.

The motel takes the edge off our high spirits. It lets us know that a nationally known brand name does not necessarily mean much. Frequently, they are locally owned franchises. A Heavenly Rest in Lubbock may be the same, inferior, or superior to a Heavenly Rest in Pendleton. The one in Lubbock is a dump with worn carpeting, worn furniture, worn plumbing, and an air of neglect. There are few other guests.

We are reminded of a time when in the heat of new love, we stopped in a dusty, poverty-stricken small town in south Texas, unable to go another foot without getting between the sheets somewhere. Anywhere. We checked into the Cloud Nine Motel (actual name). Even with squeaky bed springs and a noisy window air conditioner and cockroaches, it seemed every bit as nice as the George V. And the George V wouldn't have had a view of Seventh Heaven Motel (actual name) across the road.

Out some seventy miles past Lubbock, we stop for gas in Muleshoe (actual name) and enjoy one of the pleasures of driving a well-restored '71 Westie.

While I'm pumping gas, a woman about my age comes across the driveway to take a look inside. We get to talking, and she tells me she and her first husband had owned a '65 splitty like the one Tom and Roger had advised me not to buy. Drove it 150,000 miles. Camped all over the country. Her face takes on a look I will see repeatedly when people reminisce about van life they have known – wistful, dreamy, head cocked a little to the side, eyes looking off into the distance, seeing what she alone can see.

Her current husband isn't as enthusiastic about old vans as she is, but something about ours gets him talking, too. He grew up in Austin's Bryker Woods neighborhood, which is near our condo. His grandfather was on the City Council for some years. When he had proposed a major bypass around the outer edge of Austin, he had encountered skepticism. Austin would never be big enough to need anything like that. But eventually the road was built and named Ben White Boulevard for my new friend's grandfather. It's now an urban highway with many, many lanes and access roads. It's the kind of transportation excess Ann and I and many people have reservations about, but Ben White III is proud, and I resist saying "boy, that thing's a nightmare, isn't it."

As we're talking, a dirty pickup truck with dual wheels on the rear and a couple of dogs and some tools in the bed turns off the road and pulls up close-by. The driver pushes back his sweat-stained Purina cap and stares. "Great van," he says, shaking his head and smiling before driving away. I had been wrong to assume that the van would elicit only negative responses from the good ol' boys in pickups.

For some while after leaving the gas station, we pass by feed lots where great crowds of cattle are being fattened for slaughter. The lots stink without mercy, and cramming animals so close together is cruel. If cows were a country, they would be the third largest greenhouse-gas emitter in the world. Not only that, the typical American diet with its large component of beef and other meat causes health problems. Ann shares my view; she hasn't eaten meat in forty years.

I've come a long way from idolizing my cowboy/butcher grandfather when I was a hoy and from the meat-eating way of my family. My mother liked to say that she wouldn't know to make a meal that didn't include meat. Unwillingness to eat the flesh of animals raised for slaughter was one of a number of conflicts with my family that I couldn't work through until after their deaths.

Some miles inside New Mexico, rancor about feed lots and meat eating turns loose of us. The east central part of New Mexico is arid, vast, and desolate, with low but splendid flora – creosote bushes, sage brush, long healthy grass of some sort, and at the road's edge, small blossoming flowers in a variety of colors. I scan the horizon sentry-like in hopes of seeing some tumbling tumbleweeds, but it must be the wrong time of year.

The road stretches straight to the horizon under a seemingly endless sky with hardly a car in sight. Many people derive a sense of freedom and comfort from such unobstructed views and wouldn't like living without it. I enjoy it, but I feel equally at home with urban prospects. One time a Texas friend visiting Manhattan asked, "What do you do for sky?" To me, the midtown skyline looking south from the ball fields of Central Park offers spiritual sustenance as powerful as the sight of a majestic mountain ridge.

I suppose the shape of a road resonates, too. Living mostly among straight roads must form life in some way that is different from, say, the winding, hilly roads in the piney woods of east Texas, where I grew up. Interstates and urban spaghetti bowls do something to the spirit too. So far as I can tell, nothing good.

After a while, our long private highway gets a little hilly. Thunderheads and cloud formations put on a show off to the west and north. Approaching Albuquerque, the Sandia range rises up dramatically, though the thrill of it is marred by having to drive for a time on an Interstate. We leave it at the eastern edge of Albuquerque and drive through the heart of the city on historic Route 66 with its period motels, neon signs, and square structures of adobe or something that looks like adobe.

A second night in a second motel of the same brand as the one in Lubbock confirms that brand names mean little where motels are concerned. This South Albuquerque Heavenly Rest is way more to our liking than the Heavenly Rest in Lubbock.

We spend the evening watching a video of how to erect the clever English tent that attaches to the van. It's hard to follow. The manufacturer seems to have shipped the wrong attachment parts, and the video is for a different model of tent than the one we bought. The seller assured me that the instructions apply to both. I'm not convinced. Production values of the video are problematic too. The instructor gets between the camera and the part being illustrated, he talks too fast, and he speaks some British dialect that sounds like pig Latin. But maybe I'm just too given to anxiety (sloth and occasional grouchiness as well) to enjoy using a tent like that one. The helpful video just makes me anxious. I picture arriving at a campground at dusk or later, tired, hungry, thirsty, and cranky, all of which makes getting the thing set up a tedious, time-consuming effort that would likely fail.

That's unfortunate. We have campground reservations the next night at Mesa Verde National Park in Colorado.

CHAPTER TWELVE
MESA VERDE MISTAKE

The day starts with an email from Tom.

"Keep in touch and ... upon your return I'll finally be able to get a good night's rest. Only a phone call away.

P.S. How's the oil level?"

Nice. I wish he had been so helpful with the tent when I showed him a drawing of it. I mentioned that it looked a little complicated, hoping he would somehow make it seem easy. He's good at that kind of magic. Not this time. His response was something like, "You'll probably try it once, get really frustrated, then throw it away." Gee. Was that how it was going to be? Not a chance. It was expensive, I have four college degrees, and Ann is as stubborn as they come. By nightfall, we will be passing freely in and out of that tent at Mesa Verde.

The country from Albuquerque north to about the Colorado line is high desert. It's like east-central New Mexico in its pervasive sense of remoteness but with dramatic rock formations in the near distance and the sense of being outsiders in Indian country. Now and then, a row of two-line utility poles veers away from the highway and runs to the horizon without any discernible destination. Sometimes they stand beside empty unpaved roads; sometimes they just take off across open country.

Nearing Colorado, flat becomes hilly, and mountains are visible in the distance. The van is running well, though, so they seem more inviting than ominous. In Durango, we turn west and begin the forty-mile drive to Mesa Verde. Tent anxiety notwithstanding, we're excited about seeing the cliff dwellings and visiting the archeological museum.

Not so fast. Between Durango and Mesa Verde, we have to deal with Hesperus Pass. It's 8019 feet high, and until we reach a good part of that elevation, the weather is hot. As the engine labors, the oil temperature rises. We stop to let it cool, and a picture comes to mind of westward-bound, dustbowl Okies in beat-up old cars with boiled-over radiators. We start again after a bit and inch up the rest of the ascent at 30-35 miles an hour, keeping watch for a shoulder where we can stop again if we need to. It's our first experience with mountain passes, so we have no sense of what the van is capable of.

Finally, we reach the summit, take a deep breath, then roll easily down the twenty-three miles to Mesa Verde. Shoot. That wasn't so hard. What were we so afraid of? Still, it's clear that the van is not made for driving in mountains, and more lie on the road ahead. Some of the passes are higher than Hesperus.

The reception we get when we pull up in front of the park registration center turns us from concern about the van's limitations to pleasure in its mystique. An Asian man with two young children approaches before we even get out and begins taking pictures. He talks to the kids in a way that reminds me of an old man I once saw leading a little boy around Canterbury Cathedral telling him the stories depicted in the stained-glass windows and passing on the tenets of faith. A family hurries over excitedly because the young teenage daughter had once built a Lego model of a red VW van – just like ours, except it was a splitty. Several other people stop to admire it.

We get a map from the office and drive off to find our site. We don't have a particular one reserved; we're instructed to pick one that isn't in use and claim it as ours by posting a tag on a post by the road. We cruise around for a while, looking for just the right spot, like selecting a ready-to-eat avocado. There are plenty to choose among, but none will do. They don't have electrical connections, and as luck would have it, Ann's workflow at the moment is more demanding than usual. In the clients' views, all of it has to be finished immediately. She can work without power by using the hotspot on her iPhone and running her laptop on battery. And they can both be recharged off the van's engine, but park rules limit vehicle idling. None of that matters though, if she can't get cell phone reception, and it's spotty.

I stop near a man who is sitting beside a small fire drinking beer.

"Hey, I'm having trouble finding a site with a power hookup."

He comes right to the point. "There aren't any."

I drive us back to the office. On the way Ann tries unsuccessfully to get an internet signal. The nice lady behind the desk is as direct as the beer drinker was.

"You made a reservation in a section that has no hookups."

"Well, how about we change to a section that does have hookups."

"It's full."

Of course, it is. National Park campsites have to be reserved far in advance.

"How about the lodge?" It's a little pricey, but we'll accept that and enjoy it.

She lets me use the office landline to phone the lodge. Surprise. It has a vacancy. Problem solved. As we're finishing our transaction, I remember to ask if cats are permitted. They are not, and leaving BK alone in the van won't do. She's too old and sick for that.

I make my way back to the van. I'm glad Ann hasn't come in with me. If she had, we would both have talked at once – our way in such situations – and it might have made the nice lady behind the desk feel she was being badgered, which would have been unhelpful. As it was, I ever so subtly tried to get her to feel like our problem was her problem. It didn't get us a place to stay, but she did return the registration fee, despite it being an exception to Park rules. It may have helped that she was a cat person, and I sort of dramatized BK's being severely ill and really needing a comfortable place to lay her head for the night.

During the short walk out to the parking lot, I try to come up with a narrative that will shift blame for the situation from me to the National Park Service. The best I can manage is to emphasize how I have masterfully found a kind of silver lining to this cloud by getting our money back. My first recitation of this doesn't have quite the mollifying effect I hoped for. I persist.

"Yeah, sure. It's not a lot of money, but at least we got it back." No response.

I add, "and it was against policy." Silence.

With no internet connection so she could work, Ann had occupied herself by studying maps, giving special attention to steep grades, and thinking about the itinerary we (I, mostly) had planned. We have more Colorado mountains in front of us and then Utah. It is no country for old vans. It gives her another reason in addition to my botching the three-day holiday at Mesa Verde to wonder why she had married me. She doesn't actually say that, but I can tell she's thinking it.

We crawl back over Hesperus Pass and check into a motel in Durango. Over take-out Chinese food, I point out that we sure couldn't have enjoyed such a treat in a tent at Mesa Verde.

While she works late into the evening, BK on her lap, I study a mountain-pass directory used by truckers and put together a new course. Back south to Santa Fe, north on I-25 along the flat east side of the Rockies, then west across Wyoming to the coast. Continue staying in motels for a day or two. KOAs exist along interstates, but that kind of camping is unappealing.

So far, this adventure is not working out the way we had hoped. Just three days into it, and epiphanies are mounting.

We can't do mountains.

For Ann to work while having this kind of holiday is more challenging than we anticipated. She limits it to twenty-five or thirty hours a week but being timely with responses often requires her to do some work while chugging along in the rough-riding van.

Frequent unavailability of power and an internet signal precludes much camping.

I have too little time for writing blog posts about the trip, something I planned from the time we first thought about the trip. During the Depression, Ernie Pyle wrote a one-thousand-word column six days a week for five or six years while driving around the United States, Mexico, and Canada, and he had a drinking problem. What's wrong with me?

Hard questions come to mind.

Will obstacles make it impossible to enjoy this adventure?

Will we have time for the regular exercise we are unwilling to do without?

Will distractions prevent us from attending to the new. It's not possible even to look out the window and enjoy the scenery while studying a map or making reservations on a phone.

Will the ordinary requirements of living on the road – from keeping the van running to looking for bathrooms – allow us time and leisure to reflect? Without reflecting, we'll be merely covering ground.

CHAPTER THIRTEEN
BACKTRACKING

A moderately vigorous walk on a lovely path by a mountain stream that runs south out of Durango puts the snakes back in their basket. Morning optimism replaces the bedtime misgivings.

We drive east into higher elevation, but it's not scary high like Hesperus Pass. Dense evergreen forests alternate with scenic vistas blemished by clear-cutting. Still, ugly as the clear-cutting is, the view is unlike anything we knew in Texas, and that is the kind of thing we had come for.

After about forty-five miles, we come to Pagosa Springs, a town we know nothing about. Until we looked at a map during the breakfast scrum at the Durango La Quinta, we'd never heard of it. It was just the place on a map where we would turn south and make our way to Santa Fe. As Ann drives us past billboards that advertise the surpassing pleasure of a visit there, I look it up on my phone. And just like that, the previous evening's discontent returns.

From early on, we had in mind a clear picture of some things we wanted from the trip. We would not be pushed around by a rigid itinerary. We would stop any time we came across something interesting. We would include interludes of being naked in sun and water like we had enjoyed at various places in Europe. In Pagosa Springs, we could have enjoyed sun and water at least; it boasted three hot springs right in the center of town, but in a flagrant violation of the fundamental spirit of our adventure, we zip past the turnoff without even slowing down.

I regret this for a while, but the feeling passes when we stop at a country gas station, and we're treated to another moment of van glory. As I am pumping gas, a lady approaches at a speed that is impressive considering she would have been middle aged when the van came off the assembly line. Waving one of those cardboard throwaway cameras that have largely been replaced by smart phones, she asks excitedly if she can take a picture. I get BK out of her bed behind the driver's seat, and the three of us pose by the sliding door. In the Presbyterian Sunday School of my childhood, we used to sing "Brighten the Corner Where You Are." It turns out that's easy; just drive around in a well-restored old Westie.

A youngish couple in an expensive new convertible give us a by-then familiar once-over. Noticing our Texas license plates, the driver asks how the van fared in Texas heat. Starting from San Antonio, they had passed through the same heat as we had, and he knew the van's engine was air cooled. His interest in overheating turned me into my mother. Sometimes she talked so much you'd have to leave the room while she was still going strong. I tell them all about angel Cindy, the thermostatically controlled oil cooler fan, and moving the fuel pump off the engine block. They drive off as I was getting to the exciting part about Hesperus Pass. Too bad if I bored them. When people ask about the van, they should expect a thorough answer.

In Santa Fe, we enjoy an oxymoronic vegan supper that is typically New Mexican. Ann has a "fried in quinoa avocado taco with pickled onion plus beans and rice." I can't imagine how something is fried in quinoa, but that's what it says on the menu. Ann pronounces it "wonderful." I have *calabacita* enchiladas with a little red salsa and a little green, which are picante but not painfully so. I'm pleased about that; New Mexican hot sauce can do some damage. We go to bed happy that it's becoming possible to travel the country and not be at the mercy of fast food.

We're still feeling upbeat when we wake the next morning. We're through backtracking and are about to get pointed again in the direction of Lopez Island. All we have to do is get on Interstate 25 and go north. Santa Fe is not a big city (population about 80,000), but we still get lost between downtown and the freeway. We are directed to "just take Rodeo Drive." Somehow, we find that difficult. Perhaps we had been hasty in forgoing the use of a GPS.

At the freeway entrance, a sign points the way to Colorado Springs. We follow it and are moving along nicely, when I observe that the morning sun is on our left, which means we are going south. Colorado Springs is to the north. We apply some of our developing backtracking skills and make our way back to the freeway entrance at the end of Rodeo Drive. The sign pointing the way to Colorado Springs is right where it was earlier. We follow it again, and soon we are southbound again. I voice my concern forthrightly with words such as, "What the fuck is going on?'

Two solutions present themselves: mine and Ann's. Mine is to do whatever is necessary to get going north. If it means taking a road not on the map or breaking trail across a field, do it. Just stop going toward Albuquerque. Ann, being more willing to take instruction and do what she's told than I am, is of the view that we should just keep going south like the sign told us to until something good comes of it. Her way turns out to be better. After what seems like a long time in a carnival funhouse, the freeway does a big swooping 180-degree turn, and when we come out of it, Colorado Springs lies dead ahead – still a day's drive away – but in front of us, which is where we want it to be.

Musing on what we have been through and considering whether something in the high desert air led New Mexican highway engineers to play tricks with directions, I fail to check the fuel gauge. We get off at the first exit that has a gas station sign. A Shell station is said to be coming right up. But it isn't. Nothing comes right up, except an arrow directing us to the other side of the Interstate where another one points us north on the service road.

It soon morphs into what I guess to be a neglected section of historic Rt. 66. Along the way are a few "trading posts," which specialize in period souvenirs. In between, long-dead, rusted-out cars and farm implements suggest this is where some Okies gave up the effort to get to California. Several miles into this dark place, the paved surface turns to gravel. We turn back. It doesn't escape my notice that reversing course is beginning to happen with concerning frequency. Back on I-25, eying the gas gauge as intensely as texting teens look at their phones, we make it to the next exit, where there actually is a gas station.

From there to Colorado Springs, traffic is light and the road surface smooth. Ann is able to work, and some of the time, I push the speed up to 70 mph. I had read in the original driver's manual that it's capable of that, but until then, I haven't believed it. Maybe some freeway driving now and then will be a pleasant change.

Next morning, we drive to a local park to take a walk. On the way, the oil warning light comes on. This is not supposed to happen. All I had to do to prevent it was check the level each morning and add more if it's low. Simple. But I haven't done it, and that, plus the high-speed driving on the freeway, may have brought the new engine to a premature death.

I immediately make a sharp right onto a quiet neighborhood street, hustle around to the back and pull the dipstick, which is a more commendable accomplishment than it sounds like; it merits an old-van version of a Purple Heart Medal.

Here's what I mean. Getting to the dipstick requires raising the small top-hinged lid on the engine compartment and sticking my head in. My head shares space with the sharp ends of two protruding sheet metal screws. I do my best to ignore the blood. More bleeding comes from barking my knuckles when the tight-fitting dipstick finally comes loose. We'll be way far along in the trip before it occurs to me to put on gloves.

The dipstick appears never to have had any oil on it. I break into a sweat. Surely, I've stopped in time. I open a quart of the oil Tom had sent with us and try to open the filler cap on the engine. It's screwed on so tight and the space where it's located is so cramped, I can't get purchase on it. I know little about auto mechanics. Ann, less. She does, however, save us an embarrassing call to AAA. "Yeah, that's right. Road service. I can't get the oil filler cap off."

During her years in the food business before going to law school, Ann opened stuck lids on jars of mayo and such by running a knife around under the edge. She nudges me out of her way and jams the shortest flat-head screwdriver we have up under the edge of the filler cap and runs it around as far as space permits. That does it.

Because the filler tube is in a tight space toward the back of the compartment, I had brought along a plastic funnel with a long spout. But it's too long, and it's inflexible. For the second time in less than an hour, Ann rescues us. Her hands are smaller than mine, and she has dexterity sufficient to have decorated countless cakes, pastries, and wedding cakes. She adds almost two quarts and spills only a few drops on the engine.

Holding a bloody napkin on my head and another one on my hand, I go around and turn the key. The engine starts, *and* the warning light goes off.

For the remainder of the trip, I check the oil level every morning. We'll face another problem with oil, but it won't be caused by my negligence.

CHAPTER FOURTEEN

FROM MOTOR OIL TO CARDINAL NEWMAN

Leaving Colorado Springs, we drive staring at the oil indicator light and listening for changes in the engine's sound, but no damage is apparent, and after a while we stop worrying about it.

The pleasant driving from Santa Fe gives way to heavy traffic as we approach Denver. And the weather gets hot – hotter than I expected. I shouldn't be surprised, though. It's August, and we're on the plains east of the Rockies. So, we drive slowly keeping an eye on the temperature gauge and getting in the way of freeway traffic.

In Fort Collins, we take a break at a Whole Foods Market. Ann brings BK in with us. We get lunch and take seats in the dining area. BK quickly attracts the attention of some children who see her through the screened sides of her carrier. Ann unzips the top a little, and she pops her head out. The children are delighted by that, and so is Ann. As always, Baby Kitty brings out her quiet, easy self. Together, the two of them slow me down. The tensions of the morning release their grip.

"Her name is BK," Ann tells the kids. "It stands for Baby Kitty." It's like saying, "once upon a time." At the least encouragement, or none, one of us will recite the story it introduces. It's Ann's turn now.

"When we brought her home from a shelter, she was a tiny kitten, just old enough to get along without her mother. We already had a really big adult cat. Weighed twenty-one pounds. Named Bulldozer. So naturally we just started calling her Baby Kitty."

One of the kids says, "She's still little."

"Yes, she never did get as big as many cats, and she's skinny now because she's sick. We have to give her injections every day." The children make sympathetic faces.

* * * *

North of Fort Collins, we encounter strong wind, which will knock us around for the next few days. It comes out of the west and bangs against the side of the van. Gusts threaten to throw us off the highway. Steering demands attention and a firm grip on the wheel.

After herding the van among these side blasts for about an hour, we enter Wyoming, where we turn directly into the wind on Interstate 80. If the head wind would come steadily from one direction, it would only slow us, but it doesn't. It fluctuates a little to the right of dead ahead, then a lot to the left, gusts alternating between steady and strong and a moment or two of little or none but always more or less in front of us and pushing against the flat front of the van making the engine rev and strain and our arms tired. Signs warn that the wind sometimes reaches 45 mph. I read later that from time to time, it turns over a tractor-trailer rig. When combined with snow, the highway often becomes impassable. The wind is a living force, a constant presence, usually an adversary, always a reminder that nature is in charge.

Long sections of the highway are under construction and reduced to two lanes with no passing and no shoulder. Despite the wind, most vehicles move along at normal highway speed when their way is not blocked by that nifty-looking, restored Westie. We can't go much over 45.

The barren, slightly rolling, treeless countryside stretching uninterrupted to the horizon is "wide open space" in pure form. There is a city now and then – Cheyenne, Rawlins, Rock Springs – but little human life in between. We stop at an isolated gas station, where wind is blowing so hard, it's difficult to stand up straight while pumping gas. I enjoy a break from urban life now and then, but our crossing of Wyoming on I 80 is too much of a good thing.

Ann finishes her work shortly after leaving Ft. Collins, so we take turns fighting the wheel until we get to Rawlins. It's only three-hundred miles from where we started in the morning, but it feels like more. Fatigue and the wind make the prospect of camping unappealing, and putting up the tent in that wind would probably be impossible, even if we knew how. We stay in a Hampton Inn and keep intact our string of nights in a motel.

Ann's work, my blogging and making notes toward a book, and driving in a variety of challenging conditions is not what we had in mind when we were imagining the trip. It's disheartening. I mention this to Ann, and she agrees, but she adds, "we're away from the life we were slipping into in Austin, and that's worth a lot." I don't dispute it.

By bedtime, we are settled on a plan that began forming as we were fighting traffic and the wind: we'll take a vacation from our vacation. It strikes me uncomfortably that if we're wearing down after only six days, we might not be cut out for long adventures in a classic VW van.

A tolerable 108 miles farther west on I-25 would bring us to Rock Springs, where we could turn south and into a perhaps less battering wind, and after sixty miles, arrive at Flaming Gorge National Recreation Area. Three days at its lodge, and we'd be refreshed and ready for whatever lay ahead. We know little about Flaming Gorge; we've come across it only that evening while looking at maps. A few minutes of research makes it seem just what we need – scenic, uncrowded, historic, and with few of the resort-type entertainment activities we have aged out of.

Before setting off in the morning, I gas up and check the oil at the station next to the motel. We've driven only about three hundred miles since adding oil in Colorado Springs, but Tom told me to check it every morning, and after almost burning up the engine, I do that. When the stubborn dipstick pops loose, I open up the wound on my knuckles that has not yet begun to heal from the same action twenty-four hours earlier, but I hardly notice it; I'm dismayed by what I see on the dipstick. I turn it around this way and that to get better light on it. There's no denying it, though; it's at least a quart low. What the hell is going on? The engine is almost new. It shouldn't be burning oil at that rate.

The station doesn't have zinc-containing oil, so I buy "straight" 30-weight, which Tom said would do in a pinch. (I don't know what the "W" means in 10W-30, but Tom said don't put any W-type in the van, and that's enough for me.) Using a paper filter, I pour in a quart.

I worry the dipstick out again. It calls for more oil. That just doesn't make sense. I check for a leak, but there is nothing on the pavement. Finally, it comes to me. The oil is too colorless for the level to be readily visible on the dipstick.

I have probably overfilled the crankcase, and, O Lord, that's bad. Ann is sitting in the van checking emails and isn't aware of the crisis. I give myself a moment before I get in and see what happens when I turn the key. The engine starts, and I let it idle for a few minutes, and catch my breath. Ann continues to look at her phone. I get out and check again for leaks on the pavement. None.

I don't say anything to Ann about what I've done, and I drive to Flaming Gorge under the weight of solitary self-reproach, worst-case eventualities flitting through my mind. But we make it without a problem. Possibly, I didn't fill it completely in Colorado Springs, leaving room for what I had added in Rawlins. The next time I get a chance, I'll find out how much oil it holds when full. Until I know for sure, I'll assume that it holds more than I thought. And maybe the high-rpm driving into the headwind had used some.

At Rock Springs, we turn onto Rt 181 and drive for 65 miles, most of it alongside the ever-deepening gorge formed by the Green River. The topography is a welcome change from the flat land we were on while crossing southern Wyoming. The red sandstone of the gorge reflects sunlight dramatically, and the nineteenth century explorer,

John Wesley Hardin, gave it the name Flaming Gorge. In the 1960s, the Flaming Gorge Dam created the 91-mile-long lake, the featured attraction of the park.

The "resort" where we are going to regroup is modest; more of a fish camp actually. Our condo is a rough three rooms with a rudimentary kitchen. Acceptable, but not what "resort condo" calls to mind.

We walk over to the resort dining room for supper. America's growing demand for vegetarian/vegan offerings has not yet found its way to Flaming Gorge, so we make do with a baked potato and salad. No complaint about that. We often have the same supper at home. But we don't think of our Austin condo as a resort. It's too windy to dine on the deck. We're in bed at 8:00 and asleep shortly after.

We wake the next morning wanting to make something more satisfactory of resort life, and we do. We have a hearty breakfast of oatmeal and fruit in the resort dining room, I do my old-man calisthenics, then we take a spirit-lifting hike. Something over three miles. Slightly less wind. Not hot, not cool, just right. Meadows, hills, distant vistas, the lake glistening down in the gorge. It's delightful, but I found it pretty taxing. I'm out of breath much of the time, and have some back pain, but I take it to be just cramping caused by lack of conditioning, not anything to worry about.

It has been seven months since my back surgery, and before starting, I had considered whether my back would hold up well under the physical requirements of the trip. I decided it would, but slight anxiety about it came along for the ride.

A more worrisome issue is BK's health. When we return from our outing, she seems weaker and withdrawn. We hope she's not in pain, but just infirm and beginning to shut down. We pray Cardinal Newman's prayer for her to have "a holy rest and peace at the last." But not yet, please God.

CHAPTER FIFTEEN
ENTERING FULL-VACATION MODE

From Flaming Gorge, we drive south into Utah before turning north and making our way almost to Idaho. Mostly uninteresting. Much of it on an Interstate. Just miles to be covered. I think of E.B. White's notion that the journey itself is as important as the destination. I infer he means you should enjoy the journey. Yeah, well, he never drove hour after hour on an Interstate.

Toward the end of the day, the driving gets more interesting. We turn onto US 89/91 and enter a rich agricultural area. Roadside fruit and vegetable stands have signs promoting cherries, peaches, and apricots. I'm surprised. My picture of Utah has always been limited to mountains and salt flats, neither of which are any good for growing fruit.

We stop for lunch at a roadside park and are met by something else unexpected. Ann inadvertently leaves the sliding door of the van open, and BK hops out. She's an indoor kitty, and she likes it that way. Once when she was young, she slipped out onto the long front porch of the former monastery. We rushed out to be didn't stray too far, but we needn't have worried. When we opened the door, she raced back into the house, relieved to return to her indoor life.

This time her little excursion is different. She walks around slowly and calmly, not at all alarmed, sniffing the air, and enjoying being out. What is that about? And unlike when we came in from our hike at Flaming Gorge, she shows little sign of being sick. She's quiet and peaceful, the way she is when lying on Ann's breast at the start of every day. Has she become reconciled to her impending death? Are cats capable of that?

* * * *

Another night in a motel. This time in Logan, a place that interests us so little, I make few notes about it in my diary except that we bought a microwavable dinner for us and a new brand of treats for Baby Kitty. She likes them a lot. Eats so many she gets diarrhea. Looks perky the next morning, though, when we get on I 84 and make our way north then west across Idaho.

It's another hot, long day of driving, but it's harvest time, and even from the freeway, we participate in a way in the classic beauty of hay being cut and stacked and vegetables being picked and loaded for market.

We stop for the night in Boise, and next morning I wash the van. Later in the day, I get the oil changed. I try a VW garage that Tom recommended, but it's booked. They suggest another old-VW shop. Just guessing, I'd say there are few cities the size of Boise, population around 227,00, that offer two such shops.

They can't take me until after checkout time at the motel, though. It's a busy workday for Ann, and practicing law in the waiting room of a garage, then continuing in the Westie when we get back on the road has no appeal. So, we stay another night in Boise but in a different motel. At the first, the taps run rusty water, and it's generally down at the heels. The second is new and smells it, we're allowed to check in early, and Ann works without being distracted by her surroundings, while I go to the garage. Better.

Like Tom and Roger, these guys recommend a zinc-containing oil. They carry a German brand that in their view is superior to all others, and they proudly claim to be the only shop west of the Mississippi that sells it. I don't know why VW engines want zinc and others,

71

say Chevrolets, are indifferent to it. I just pay and leave the question unexplored, like the many possibly interesting side roads we haven't taken.

The next day, the feel of the trip changes.

We stop at a lovely, well cared-for park and have lunch in the shade of towering evergreens and ease into a slower rhythm. You wouldn't think that would be noteworthy; we're on a vacation. But not just. We have a destination, and at some level, we're eager to get to it. Everyone who was ever a child in the back seat of a car driven by Dad on any kind of holiday trip has experienced that urgency. Besides, we've been encountering so many obstacles, the fun we set out to have has been elusive.

The distance from Boise to our next stop, Pendleton, Oregon, is 221 miles, which is less than we drive on many days, and since we made an early start, we just poke along. The temperature is in the seventies. We eat lunch slowly, and afterward drive a few miles out of the way to a scenic overlook. To that point, we've done little ordinary sight-seeing. It feels good. We're finally having the trip we wanted.

When we get going toward Pendleton again, the views from the highway are altogether pleasant, varying between forested mountains and parched lower elevations with swathes of irrigated farmland showing green against tan. The Snake River flows large as we track alongside it and the historic Oregon Trail. We fancy we're having the same feeling of renewal that the weary pioneers must have felt when they got to this point.

The metamorphosis from obstacle fighters into ordinary tourists continues in Pendleton where we enjoy the slow-paced pleasure of walking around town and visiting points of interest. We learn that Pendleton is about Roundup, a famous rodeo dating from 1910, Pendleton Woolens, the Oregon Trail, the Union Pacific, and the Pendleton Underground, where Chinese railroad workers made a life below streets to escape mistreatment. Picking up bits and pieces this way is fun. And it supplies superficial introductions, which their mention in the future will ring bells of recollection.

At lunch time, we find our way to a bar for a couple of locally brewed beers and a Beyond Burger. I've heard of this vegan burger, but I've never eaten one. It turns out to be lip-smacking delicious and indistinguishable from meat, except I don't have to think about dead cows and the harms caused by the cattle industry. Ann, a vegetarian for over forty years, finds the Beyond Burger to be *too much* like meat. It will be some time before she fully enjoys one.

She has a little work to finish in the evening, but despite that, we continue in relaxed mode. I read *The Old Ways* by Robert Macfarlane, a riveting book about classic hikes and trails in Britain and elsewhere. We end the evening watching *Sullivan's Travels*, a film Ann published a critical essay on when she was a film-history student. I've never seen the movie. After I do, I understand why she has liked it so much for so long.

CHAPTER SIXTEEN
GHOSTS

It's the first time either of us have seen the Columbia River, which, it turns out, is mighty like the Mississippi but with clear water. Until we learned this, all we knew about it was a couple of verses of Woody Guthrie's song. We sing them as it rolls on and we drive over it.

In Washington, we turn west on Rt 14, a scenic route, which runs along mostly within sight of the river. Two lanes. Little traffic. Sparsely populated. Rolling. Orchards. Lots of vineyards and wineries, including the massive holdings of the Chateau St. Michelle winery.

I once lived in central Washington on the east slope of the Cascades, but I never made it down here. I'm so enjoying the look of it, I pay too little attention to a sign that warns "next services 63 miles."

Some while after passing the sign, I discover that the needle on the gas gauge is on empty. It does not escape my notice that this is a repeat of what had happened back in Colorado. I slow down and begin studying the road ahead for one of those gas-station signs that stick up every so often alongside most highways. Not this one, though. Occasionally, a farm truck passes us going the opposite direction, but there few other signs of life.

As the gas supply dwindles to what must be the last teaspoon, a crossroad appears. Not much of one – just a ribbon running north from down by the river through sloping acres of grapevines. And there, like the water-bearing angel, Cindy, are two old and dusty fuel pumps – one gasoline, one diesel. No attendant. No convenience store. No brand name. No advertising material. The pavement around the pumps is badly in need of repair.

A small sign says something unclear about the pumps being for commercial use. Well, I'm writing blog posts about this adventure hoping I can turn them into a book. That will have to pass for "commercial." Anyway, there's no one around who might say it does not qualify. I find a slot to insert a credit card, and it works.

In the future, I will come to doubt that those pumps actually existed. The notes in my diary are vague, and I can't find a credit card charge for the purchase of gasoline or anything else along that highway on that day. I suppose the charge must be there on some other day or the merchant was called something that doesn't look like a gasoline retailer. I don't search exhaustively, though; I like the possibility of the pumps not being there. Whatever happened, we drove on without running out of gas.

After an hour or so we come to Mayhill State Park, which we find to be altogether inviting. Leafy, but with plenty of open sky. Clean rest rooms. A roped-off swimming area in the river. A herd of giggling, squealing children. And tent campers.

The tents trigger a Hickey moment. In college, I once performed the role of Hickey in a reading of O'Neill's *The Iceman Cometh*. Day after day, Hickey says he's going to leave the saloon where he seems to live. But he never does. He and his drinking buddies stay on interminably, nourishing themselves with beer and illusions. It's time for me to stop being Hickey and shake off the nice-motel habit and be like the carefree campers near our picnic table and start sleeping on the ground under a canvas roof. But not yet. We have a reservation for the next two nights at a Hampton Inn suite with a view of the Columbia.

We recross the Columbia and enter the small town of Hood River. From the bridge, majestic Mt. Hood, elevation 11,250, is visible to the southwest. The river below is off-putting, though. It's a hive of sail boarders, parasailers, and personal-watercraft jockeys. They're young and overprivileged and bent on pleasure. Nothing wrong with having a good time, but it's easy for me to think that for them, having a good time is just about everything. They make the Columbia River Gorge National Scenic Area seem like the Columbia River Gorge National Hedonism Center. If not quite that, it is at least unlikely that they are doing much nature study or delving into history. Still, the natural beauty of the gorge – even as a party venue – is spectacular.

In the evening, we walk along the river to a pizza restaurant, which is crowded with the oh-so self-assured young people who had been playing in the water. It sells vegan pizza, good local beer, and, implausibly, T shirts with a picture on the front of a classic red Westie. I can't make sense of that. The young pizza eaters crowding up to the bar are BMW people. They are surely an unpromising market for such shirts. They were not alive during the Age of Aquarius. Probably know little about it. Other than weed and casual sex they have nothing in common with the braless, bearded, idealistic, war resisters for whom the VW van possessed almost numinous force. It's too loud in the bar for me to pursue an explanation.

In the motel, we put on our new shirts and eat pizza. Like all the vegan pizzas I've tried, it bears little resemblance to real pizza – actually, little resemblance to anything you'd want to eat. But I'm pleased that veganism is becoming so popular.

Next morning, Ann works, and I welcome the opportunity to walk alone. Lately, when walking with Ann, I've been having minor back pain similar to what had preceded the last surgery. I'm guessing it's because her default pace is faster than mine. Alone, I move along at my natural pace, something between a mosey and a saunter, and I have no pain. I'm relieved. A week or so of slow walking and more attention to the exercises I was taught in post-op therapy, and I'll be able to keep up with her again. It's a happy thought.

It's a Zip-a-Dee-Doo-Dah day. Temperature in the seventies. Light breeze. Low humidity. Cloudless, cornflower blue sky. When I left the motel, BK was looking perkier, a result, I suppose of still another kind of kitty food. Hood River is a different place from the one I entered the afternoon before. Children play, dogs chase balls, and people sit quietly on benches, drinking coffee and soaking up sun.

On the way out of town, we stop at a farmers' market crowded with displays of locally grown fruits and vegetables. We walk every aisle pointing at these greens, asking about those melons, immersed in the elemental pleasure of food just harvested, much of it with dirt still on it. It calls up memories of markets we've known in Provence and England and other places. We were often traveling on those occasions, and, lacking a kitchen, we bought only what we could eat without cooking, usually just cheese and fruit. So it is that day in Hood River.

I give myself a break from veganism and after much dithering select a small block of cheddar, then turn my attention to fruit. And there they are: Red Haven peaches. I've not seen a Red Haven since I grew them in my yard in central Washington in the early seventies. I liked them more than any kind of peach I'd ever had.

I grew vegetables too. Unlike the fruit trees, which were mature when we bought the house, they required my agency. One day when I thought the hard winter was over, I spaded up a plot in the back yard and started planting English peas. My neighbor stuck his head up over the fence and warned me that it was too early to plant. I didn't listen; the snow had melted, and the ground had thawed. But he was right. The first shoots got buried in snow. I planted again, and it snowed again, but this time the plants were a little further along, and the snow didn't kill them. They yielded a big crop, excellent in taste, appearance, and size. I wondered if I had stumbled onto a new, improved way to cultivate peas – plant before winter is fully finished.

Encountering the Red Havens has opened the curtain on another existence, one of immeasurable size and outside the limitations of time. The same thing had happened on the bridge, when I looked down on those young people playing in the river. In an instant, I lived several years of life as the person I was at their age, mine admirable, theirs objectionable. In less time than it took to cross the bridge, I and my college friends were protesting the misbegotten war and working to end segregation and reading poetry and having a go – unsuccessfully in my case – at Kierkegaard and being earnest and seeking. Not all of us, of course. Not any of us all the time. At some point, I will become less judgmental and realize that if I hadn't been self-supporting and always short of money, I would have been a lot like those parasailers who set me off. But that will be a while coming.

Old people are derided for living in the past, and especially for telling the same stories over and over. We can be tiresome, but if it isn't overdone, there is much to be said for looking backward in old age. Mulling over "what was it all about?" can lead to peace or something close to it. And recitation of history, including personal history, can be of benefit to the young. Anyway, for good or ill, a long trip in a classic VW camper will evoke some reliving and rethinking. It may be the best reason to make such a trip.

The Hood River Red Havens are disappointing. Poor texture and not much taste. I don't know what to make of that. Maybe I've gotten hold of a bad batch at the market. Maybe the ones that grew in my yard were not as good as I remember.

CHAPTER SEVENTEEN
CHANCE ENCOUNTER

High above the Gorge, cars are parked willy-nilly along the shoulder of Scenic Route 30. Roadside overlooks are crowded with pedestrians, selfie sticks on high.

It's time for popular natural attractions to adopt something like the conveyor belt that moves people past the English crown jewels, or admission times like at art exhibits, or a lottery system like some states use to limit the number of hunters on public land. Rationing of campsites is already in effect; there are only so many places to park a van or pitch a tent. But that limited number often seems too high, and it doesn't limit drive-through traffic or hiking that starts from outside campgrounds.

When we emerge from Rt. 30 at its west end, I feel about the same as I do after being in heavy traffic anywhere and not at all refreshed by the time we've just spent in spectacular natural beauty.

My annoyance grows when we enter Portland, but not because it's overcrowded. It's a city of 648,000. We knew that, and we like cities, crowds and all. (Crowds in cities – good; crowds in parks – bad.) But we don't know our way around this city, streets are not in a grid, we are no good at using our smartphone directional aids, and we have a reservation at a downtown hotel (talk about not camping), which we can't find. Eventually, there it is – not where we expected, either – just *there*. It was as if the god of urban traffic decided to stop messing with us.

My plan is to park temporarily in the loading zone, lug a couple of suitcases and BK up to our room, then drive to the hotel garage, take the stuff off the roof, and lock it inside. It's not to be. Valet parking is required, so I have to unload the luggage rack in the street while trying not to get clipped by passing traffic.

In the room, I realize I've left BK's Lactated Ringers and syringes in the van. I wouldn't mind going to get them – a little walk would smooth me out – but only valets (priests) are allowed to enter the garage (the sacred space behind the rood screen). I can't remember where I squirreled away the meds, so I give the valet an even bigger tip than I had given him a few minutes earlier and plead with him to keep looking till he finds them. After almost an hour, he returns, smiling triumphantly. I think he's pleased to have been given an assignment of such moment.

Ann and I take a walk and a deep breath. The park along the Willamette River in the city center is all green grass and tall trees. On side streets, there are lots of the homeless people and camps that Portland is known for, a result, I speculate, of a relatively mild climate and the tolerant – non-punitive, at least – attitude of the famously liberal city. A few blocks from the hotel, white nationalists mill around in something resembling a parade. Reportedly, they've come mostly from out of town to make a television-worthy objection to Portland's progressivism. Surprisingly, they seem cheerful and good-humored. Maybe it's the mellowing influence of Portland culture and Portland pot.

Next day, we enjoy a perfect Sunday lunch. Two hours at a quiet sidewalk table. For me, another break from veganism – smoked salmon and Caesar salad. Excellent local wine. A delightful conversation with a gay couple at the next table. One is African-American, the other white.

The lunch plays against a background of a joyous civic event in which for several hours on summer Sundays, automobile traffic is limited or banned completely on downtown streets and in other parts of the city to make way for bicycles. Hundreds of riders stream by a few feet from our table. Old and young, Some in costumes. On tandems. On tricycles. Slowly. Quietly. Radiating bonhomie. Volunteer monitors like school crossing guards help pedestrians cross the flow.

One of the men is from Houston, the other a life-long resident of Portland. We talk about differences between living in Texas and Oregon. We discover shared values and tastes. It's refreshing and affirming.

In the morning paper, I had read a column about the beauty of traditional liturgy with its rich symbolism, special language, and whole-hearted embrace of mystery. In the columnist's view, Christianity is in the early stage of return to that form of worship. The guitar Masses and make-it-up urge spawned by Vatican II are becoming less dominant. I would like to talk about this with these congenial new acquaintances. With anyone actually. But it's likely they will be indifferent or hostile, almost certainly uninformed; most people are. Besides, God talk can be as intimate as sex, and we've only just met.

Almost fifty years earlier, I had attended an Anglo-Catholic Mass in Portland. I was an Episcopalian, but at the time, the elaborate ritual that is the Anglo-Catholic way was not part of my devotional practice. I'd read about it, and I'd seen it in films, but I'd never lived where it was available. I was confirmed at All Saints Episcopal Church in Austin. Shortly after, I moved to Baghdad, where I attended services at St. George's Anglican Church. It followed traditional forms, but it was not at all high church. Still, I liked it well enough, and its rituals and language were almost indistinguishable from those of my home parish. But when I returned to Austin a couple of years later, revision of the *Book of Common Prayer* was underway. I didn't care for the new way and the fiddling around with variations. I still don't. While I wasn't looking, my church had moved worship in the direction of blandness and rationality. I wanted Mass, the Daily Office, and the sacraments to manifest the ineffable mystery that is the presence of God. So, when I visited the church in Portland, I was enthralled by the Anglo-Catholic way.

We do talk with our new friends about where we and they have lived and which places we have liked and disliked. Ann and I recall our years in London as exceptionally satisfying. We could be happy living there again, maybe even for the rest of our lives. Hong Kong and Zurich were interesting but objectionable in various ways. And Austin is not working out for us. We've lived in Austin off and on ever since attending the University, but now we're having trouble feeling at home there. We are in but not of Texas, and although Austin is in various ways an oasis, it's still in Texas.

Our new friends seem interested, so Ann and I run on with this line. Of all the places we've lived, we've felt most at home in New York City, especially Manhattan. Ann has some roots there. Her parents and grandparents were New Yorkers, though she grew up in Texas. I have no New York roots. Either way, we had been enchanted by it from an early age. And like millions of new arrivals, we immediately became naturalized New Yorkers. New York is definitively cosmopolitan, so newcomers like us can be completely at home there.

I leave out the part about New York making it possible for us to be Anglo-Catholics, about the parish of St. Ignatius of Antioch with its asperges and plainsong, its belief in the Real Presence of Christ in the eucharist, its openness to female priests and openly gay priests, its celebration of same-sex marriage in the same way as marriage between a woman and a man, its diverse congregation.

It is a rapid, ramble of a conversation, and at some point, we get going on Sabbaticalhomes.com, which Ann has recently discovered. It's a sort of VRBO through which college faculty rent their homes to other college faculty, current or past, and I qualify. The offerings are relatively affordable and are located in interesting towns and cities all over the world: both Cambridges, Brisbane, Cape Town, just about anywhere there is a college or university. Rental periods vary from a few days to a year or more. Maybe the program will make it possible for us to come to terms with Texas and our restlessness by occasional long stays in New York or London. At this point, we are talking more to ourselves than to our new friends at the next table, but they tolerate it well.

The conversation gives us a lot to think about while walking back to the hotel. It opens up a sense of possibly moving onto some new way of being.

We don't know it at the time, but we are approaching clarity about who we are and where we have to live.

It's still on my mind as BK and I enjoy a most satisfactory nap. Afterward, I read until bedtime, Baby Kitty on my lap, sleeping peacefully, twisted into a knot the way kitties do. She seems to be more peaceful than usual. Maybe I'm imagining that. I hope not.

CHAPTER EIGHTEEN
JUST A PET?

A vague sense of a new and more satisfactory life joins us for coffee. We'll start it in a small way by actually camping tonight at Grayland State Park on the Pacific coast of Washington. We'll continue camping for several more days as we make a circuit of the Olympic Peninsula.

In Seaside, Oregon, we stop at midmorning to buy camp food – canned beans, pancake mix, and the like – plus a baguette, plant-based cheese, hummus, and a tomato for lunch, which we enjoy at a city park in Astoria.

The drive along the coast takes longer than expected, and as it gets later, wind and mist come up, and the call of clean sheets and a comfortable bed wins out again.

We're beginning to feel like frauds for still not having done any camping in the campervan. Before starting the trip, we had talked up the wonders of the expensive tent to friends and family. Returning to Austin and having to admit that it was an unrealistic plan and being laughed at is beginning to seem like a real possibility.

It shouldn't be this way. In college, Ann spent a summer riding a bicycle around Europe, mostly alone, pitching her tent every night, no matter the circumstances. In Scotland, it rained every day for two weeks. Once she was surprised to wake up on a soccer field. As a boy, I did plenty of tent camping among the bugs and snakes and wild pigs in the piney woods of East Texas. Later in life in the Jordanian desert, in the Cascade Mountains, and on beaches. Ann and I once spent several days in a tent during summer on the Texas coast; for purifying, dehydrating, punishing heat, you can't beat it. But now, it seems we may have outgrown tent camping.

It's high tourist season, and the towns along the shore are small, so finding a room is difficult. It's dark when we check into the only place available, a Best Western in Ocean Shore. It's generally unpleasant.

In the morning, Ann discovers millipedes or something of the sort coming up through the bathtub drain. BK vomited in the night, and she has diarrhea. Has she eaten one of the disgusting creatures? Ann thinks she's wheezing and looking weaker. I don't quite see what Ann sees. BK's just, maybe, displaying the same listlessness that has been with her off and on since before we left Austin. She does seem oddly more affectionate; she slept most of the night on my chest instead of at the foot of the bed as she usually does.

We get going without breakfast or taking any exercise, not even a short walk. It's an inhospitable place. Best to leave quickly and get on up the road.

The western and northern edges of the Olympic Peninsula are dramatic and beautiful beyond expectations. We spend the day driving slowly on a narrow winding road bordered by steep mountains that come down to the sea. But as time passes, it becomes increasingly difficult to enjoy the beauty around us. It's undeniable; BK is not doing well. Her weight loss has become alarming, and she's not moving much. Ann drives much of the day, and BK sleeps on my lap, something she rarely does in the van.

We arrive in Port Angeles at around 3:30, giving us plenty of time to set up the tent and start a planned three-day stay at a KOA, which we'll use as a base for exploring the Olympic National Forest. But first we'll find a veterinarian. An extra boost of hydration might be all that is necessary to get BK perked up. We stop at the first vet's office we come to, but they are too busy to see her. They give us directions to another one.

A kind and able young Dr. Rachel sees BK immediately. She and an assistant take her to another room to examine her and administer some tests.

After a time, they return carrying BK swaddled in a soft quilt with only her head showing. At this point in countless such narratives, the beloved pet transforms from animal to a human-like creature with emotions and thoughts and the ability to communicate them. With her eyes, Baby Kitty offers us benediction. "It's OK. Don't worry."

And then Dr. Rachel begins the awful message.

Her kidneys are hardly functioning, and she is severely dehydrated. Surely that can be treated? Well, yes. But she also has leukemia and a mass in her abdomen that is probably cancer. For a few minutes we talk possible treatments, but not seriously. It's just some words to allow us breathing space. We know what has to be done.

Dr. Rachel explains the procedure, and we agree to it. So does Baby Kitty. She is unusually calm. Accepting. Perhas even welcoming.

They take her away again to sedate her and make the necessary preparations. Ann and I wait, unmoving, numb, not talking. They bring Baby Kitty back on a cushion and wrapped in the same quilt. A festive decorative tape holds a needle in place on a front paw.

We are offered as much time as we want, just the three of us, alone. We hold Baby Kitty and stroke her for a few minutes, then signal Dr. Rachel to come back in. She kneels in front of us and speaks words of comfort. And then it's time. Baby Kitty looks into our eyes with an unmistakable message. "I'm OK with this. It's time." Cardinal Newman's prayer for a safe lodging, a holy rest, and peace at the last has been answered. That makes saying goodbye less painful, but it's still as hard as the death of a loved one always is.

Young Dr. Rachel embraces us and holds us for a long time.

The death of a pet is complicated. You're surrounded by a common attitude, which you feel though it's not spoken. The creature was "just" a cat, just a dog or parakeet or horse, so what's all that grief about? No one who has actually lost a pet takes that view.

For almost seventeen years, Ann has seldom opened her eyes in the morning without finding Baby Kitty on her breast. She spent so much time on Ann's lap while she worked, she probably could have passed the bar exam. Ann is a self-identified grouch, but never, ever, not once, did she get grumpy or annoyed at that kitty. I usually enjoy an afternoon nap. and Baby Kitty almost always joined me. If I got busy with something, she would seek me out and all but motion with her head toward the bed. She did the same when it was time to have a cocktail and watch the news in the evening.

Just a pet? Not at all.

CHAPTER NINETEEN
KEEPING ON

We check into the first motel we come to after leaving the vet's office and cancel the KOA reservation. On the way out of town, we drop off Baby Kitty's food, toys, carrier, and drugs.

The pleasure of being in that beautiful part of the world hardly registers as we move on; we are grieving.

In hopes of distraction, we turn off the highway and follow a sign to a beach. To me, "beach" means sand. This beach is rocks, small, medium, and large, what the British call shingle. To walk on it is to stumble and stagger. Still, the sun is shining, and Puget Sound is quietly picturesque.

A little farther along, a sign announces a state park. Thinking it might offer a hiking trail, we give it a try. Five miles through dense forest, the road becomes increasingly rough. Then a sign warns STEEP GRADE. ROAD NARROWS. The road is already only slightly wider than the van. We give up on finding the park.

Turning the van around without power steering in such a confined space is difficult. A couple of feet forward, muscle the steering wheel around as far as it will go, a couple of feet in reverse, over and over. I drive and Ann takes up a sentry post to warn me when I'm about to back into the steep drop-off on one side of the track

A day in Mt. Rainier National Park is enjoyable but understated and not as spectacular as we expected. For the last few miles to the park entrance, we're immersed in grayness and drizzle, moving slowly on two-lane blacktop in a lane of tall trees. It's surprisingly pleasant, almost energizing, not oppressive the way such conditions often are. It has the feel of a place where dreams and stories live.

Two easy walks in the dense evergreen forests around Longmire Meadow near where the ascent up Rainier begins are refreshing, and the rustic lodge and outbuildings constructed by the CCC bear gratifying witness to the good that can come from government spending. We never do get a view of Rainier.

From there, it's up Interstate 5 in heavy traffic to Seattle, where we'll spend a few days. I have happy memories of Seattle from decades earlier. I'm eager to see how my recollections hold up. Ann has never been there, and she's keen to see it.

We follow our usual practices when visiting a new place. First, stay in some sort of housekeeping accommodation. Then, check out local produce and beer. Cook some of it, drink some of it, dine out not much. Take in some tourist attractions. Walk a lot, some of it aimlessly. (In Seattle, the steep hills defeat us at times.) Learn how to use public transportation and enjoy the small sense of accomplishment that comes from that. Engage strangers in conversation that is more or less about the nature of life in that place. Tease in our minds the recurring question: is this the spot on earth where we could find contentment, maybe even fulfillment? We are at a point in our lives where the question is never far away, and it's a little closer to the surface since the conversation over lunch in Portland.

Seattle includes visits with old friends. One of them is about to become "someone I used to know." Apprehension and eagerness hold hands as the moment of first meeting draws near. Has the passage of time cut off the possibility of taking up where we left off? Is what we once had going to remain forever then and never now?

We needn't have worried. Ann has never met my old friend Bob, but she likes him, and he likes her. I've met Bob's second wife, Margot, but I've spent little time with her. She and Ann get on well. I fear Bob and I may have bored them. "Remember singing in the University

A Cappella Choir...Oh she died several years ago...Do you still play tennis?" All the elements necessary for an awkward, unpleasant lunch are present, but it doesn't happen. Not at all.

Ann, too, has old friends in Seattle – two sisters from her childhood in Port Arthur. Becky is married to Mike, who has a debilitating illness that requires her sacrificial devotion. We knew Mike slightly when he was healthy. Sister Molly, a retired physicist who still plays tennis and piano, is married to Sylvia, a charming Ph.D. biologist, also retired. I've never met either of them. Conversation flows as readily as if we were close friends who see each other regularly. It's a delightful evening. We drive away wishing we could do it again before too long.

The sun had come out shortly after we left Rainier, and contrary to what we expected, it doesn't rain once during the week we're in Seattle. Our apartment is on high ground and offers a sweeping view of the bay. It has a deck that circles in front of the other units on our floor, and I spend a good deal of time on it taking the sun, reading, and wool gathering.

Early one morning, while I'm on the deck drinking coffee, a cat ambles through the door I've left open and goes over to say hello to Ann. It is so like mornings with Baby Kitty, it might have upset Ann. Instead, she welcomes the visit. She thinks BK may have sent the neighbor kitty as a reminder of past blessings. For several days, I try to entice her back for longer visits, but she won't come. She stays by the door of her apartment sunning herself and ignoring me. Kitty tough love. She has given us our full allotment of reassurance; going forward, we are on our own.

CHAPTER TWENTY
WAITING FOR THE FERRY

At Anacortes, about an hour north of Seattle, we take a ferry to Lopez Island, the main event of the trip – ten days in a secluded, east-facing house perched high above the water, walking, cooking locally-grown vegetables, reading, drinking coffee naked on the porch at sunrise, and pressing our emotional reset buttons.

Waiting for the ferry, I walk along the shingle at the water's edge like I did several times in the early 1970s. On one occasion, as light was fading, I heard singing coming from a house on a bluff on the other side of a channel. A tenor of some merit performed an operatic aria I no longer recall the name of. When he finished, there was applause and the buzz of conversation. I heard – or imagined I did – the faint tinkle of ice in glasses. I was struck with longing as strong as sudden illness. I would *have* to be one of those people. They were not bound by the mundane.

The sounds called forth something already in me, a cantus firmus that goes unnoticed much of the time then unexpectedly flares into prominence.

The first time this occurred, I was fourteen or fifteen. Two college students made a presentation to my church youth group about their experience with an organization called Church World Service. They served in work camps in India during summers. Their talk was a conversion experience. Not a religious conversion, though; that would have been impossible. I had never been other than a believer, nor have I since. It was more like baptism; I was marked and signed forever as one whose delight is in ideals of service and charity and, please God, without geographic limitations. Wow. India.

The next summer, or maybe it was the summer after, I was further encouraged in that way when – unsolicited – I received the surpassingly generous gift of a European tour that included a meeting in Paris of the World Council of YMCAs, where I met people from all over the globe. At the plenary sessions, we wore earphones for simultaneous translation.

En route, the group I traveled with stopped in New York City for a few days. We explored Central Park, took the subway to a Dodgers game at Ebbets Field, and went to the top of the Empire State Building. From that point on, New York City was a part of my being.

When it was time for college, formative gifts kept coming. I enrolled at the University of Texas, a distinguished institution that had the additional virtue of charging no tuition. My parents offered encouragement, but more than slight financial support was not possible. I worked, and I managed, and I received unasked-for aid, financial and otherwise. A friend gave me a ride to Austin, got me a job waiting tables at a sorority house to go with my other job at a dry-cleaning shop. He pointed the way to an elite liberal-arts program in which a gifted teacher, Willis Pratt, opened up the joy of literature, especially Keats and the romantic poets.

I was so inspired by John Kennedy that immediately upon graduating, my then wife and our new baby and I went to Washington. I *had* to find a way to be part of the new world Kennedy was creating. A low-level position at the Peace Corps headquarters let me participate slightly, but before long, it seemed that there must be a better way to become fully me.

We returned to Texas, where for a time I thrashed around trying to find a vocation, but it eluded me, as it would for many years to come. Decades even. And when it finally arrived, it was not marked as a discrete event, it had accrued gradually.

A responsible father and husband would have just gotten a job and made the best of it. That's what my father had done at the beginning of the depression. After his death in middle age, so did my mother. They didn't concern themselves with whether they were well suited to whatever work they could get or even whether they liked it. They just did it. For reasons that I've never understand fully, I could not.

And I was tormented in ways that extended beyond finding a vocation. The country was consumed by the civil rights movement, the Vietnam war, feminism, and the counterculture. I and my friends were fervently progressive. My parents and grandparents were not.

They were of a time when being a WASP was to be superior without qualification, and not just in their minds. It was a tacit understanding in Okie culture. Their world was populated by niggers, dagos, and kikes. Catholics and Baptists were a lower order of being. In Muskogee, where I had been supremely content, the woman who came to iron our clothes and clean our little house, had to use the back door, and she called me before I was old enough to go to school "Mr. Paul." My slightly older brother was "Mr. Bobby." Facing up to this, I was distressed beyond measure; my parents and grandparents continued to think of that way as in the natural order of things. We were on opposite sides of a great national divide. I found it insupportable.

I sought help from a psychiatrist. I can't recall how well that was working before the process went terribly wrong.

My father was diagnosed with incurable cancer two days before President Kennedy was assassinated. I was living in Dallas, where there was said to be some glee about this event that I found sad beyond measure. My anguish grew accordingly.

I was alienated from my community, my family, and myself.

I was persuaded by my doctor that it would be helpful if I took a time-out as an inpatient at a hospital that he and his partners owned. Just sign myself in, and anytime I wanted, I could sign myself out. He lied to me. What followed was a locked ward, electroshock treatment three times a week, insulin shock twice a week. For three months. I tried to escape, but two white-coated orderlies ran me down, syringes in hand, before I was out of sight of the building. Nobody runs well when they're full of Thorazine.

When I was released, I was so addled, I had to relearn the values of coins; they might as well have been Tibetan. I was told the memory loss caused by the shock treatments was temporary. At best, it became spotty. Some experiences I'm said to have participated in are entirely missing from my recollection. Others, such as working at the Peace Corps, are hazy.

I did get out of the hospital in time to visit my father before he died, but not in time to come to terms with our differences.

The hospitalization may have helped me be less alienated and conflicted, but I'm not a good judge of that. Mostly, it made me feel ashamed. Only now, am I managing not to feel the stigma of it.

(Subsequently, my psychiatrist and his wife, a staff psychologist, died of a fall from their high-floor apartment. It was not an accident. Whether they had a suicide pact or it was a murder-suicide was not reported in the news coverage I saw. I've not pursued an answer.)

When I became functional again, I began graduate study in English at the University of Texas. Part way through, another unsolicited gift came along – teaching at the University of Baghdad, an experience of extraordinary fullness. I would have liked it to last much longer, but the Six Day War put an end to it.

This improbable progression of events had formed me when I stood at the ferry landing fifty years earlier and heard the aria from across the water. At the time, I was living in a small town in central Washington teaching at a state college and being uncooperative enough to get myself fired and learning that I prefer living in cities. I was still restless, still finding my way. It's no wonder the singing was so evocative.

Walking at the water's edge now while waiting for the ferry, I am visited by some of the same dense cluster of reflections and feelings that the music had brought on fifty years earlier, but this time, it's not full-blown painful longing. Ann and I have had a life much like the one I had so longed for then. Not entirely, but it seems we may be nearing the end of the long journey to peace and reconciliation.

On Lopez Island, we will think about where we have been and who we are going to be when we grow up

CHAPTER TWENTY-ONE
ON LOPEZ

I have happy memories of the San Juan Islands, but I've never been to Lopez. Ann has not been to any of the islands. We are both eager to go. We picture Lopez as small, quiet, beautiful, remote, charming, perhaps a little quaint, with seals and sea vistas and a slow pace.

Something like that is how the island presents itself on the internet. "Lopez is 15 miles long with 63 miles of shoreline and 2,500 year-round residents," and it's "perfect for travelers looking to disconnect from the distractions of urban living."

On the way to the ferry landing, we stop at a NAPA store for Turtle Wax and polishing cloths. Not since I bought a 1932 Studebaker on my fourteenth birthday have I felt the urge to wax a car. But we have to take care of the van; we don't just own it; we're stewards of a bit of history. Anyway, we're going to have plenty of leisure, and waxing the van seems like a pleasant enough way to spend an afternoon. It's not something the tourism office pitches as a fun thing to do while visiting Lopez: it doesn't list hiking, sea kayaking, fishing, and car waxing. But never mind.

We also lay in some vegan food, since it's unlikely we'll find nondairy "cheese," plant-based meat substitutes, prepared vegan entrees, and the like on the island. We do, though. Soon after unpacking, we go to a shop, which turns out to be a sort of miniature Whole Foods Market. I consider notifying the island's website that the island is not entirely free of urban distractions. But I guess "urban distractions" refers only to bad urban, such as congestion and air pollution, not to good urban like availability of organic and vegan food.

Then, it's on to the island bookstore. It's tiny, but it has any number of books I'm tempted to buy. I settle on a collection of essays about walking in the rain in England. The subject is enticing, and the blurbs are persuasive, but it turns out to be a virtuoso rendering of mismanaged adjectives. The people who wrote the blurbs were either blood relatives of the author or victims of extortion. I also buy *One Square Inch of Silence* by an acoustic environmentalist who drove a VW van across country recording the sounds he encountered and reflecting on noise. For my brain and taste, it's a bit dense with technical stuff, and I've not finished it, but I intend to; someone who has recorded the sound of a butterfly's wings is worth reading.

Lopez has a pharmacy and chartered seaplane service for medical emergencies. It seems that rural life doesn't always conform well to the stereotype.

We are pleased, however, to find much on the island that is non-urban.

We enjoy a three-hour walk starting on a paved road, which has almost no traffic. After a bit, the pavement turns into a private unpaved track, and before long we're lost. Not a lot lost but still lost. It's lovely. Intermittent views of the Sound. Heavily forested hills just beginning to show signs of autumn. Cultivated fields. Stillness limited only by an energetic mixed-breed Labrador retriever who joins us a few hundred yards from our house. His collar bears the name "Shylo," but it has no address or phone number. He circles around us and runs the whole time we're out. Ann and I get tired before we finish. Shylo doesn't.

We get our bearings after a while and make our way back toward where we started. I guess we look pretty knackered. About a mile from home, a car drives by, then after a bit, stops and backs up. The driver, a woman who lives near the house we're renting, offers us a ride. We accept – all three of us. She knows Shylo; he's a neighbor, too. Likes to roam, she says. When we let him out at his house, we meet his owners.

They take little notice of Shylo having gone with us. There's no sign of a pen or any other way to restrain him. I can't recall the last time I saw a dog left to roam free. Definitely not an urban thing.

Along the way, we buy apples and vegetables at an honor-system farm stand. We eat some of the apples on the way home. In the evening, we make vegetable soup. With the apples that are left, Ann makes a pie. We eat the whole thing with coffee on the deck while watching a ferry pass in the fading light of the setting sun. The long walk makes consuming a whole pie – it wasn't as big as some – at one meal seem less excessive. Maybe even mete and right.

We talk about whether we might come back the next summer. The day has included much that we require of a proper holiday. Reading, exercise, healthy, delicious food, friendly exchanges with people and animals, scenery to "make glad the heart of man." The usual question flitckers like heat lightning. Could we make a home on Lopez? Of course not. The island, like everyplace we've lived other than London and New York, lacks at least one essential element.

We go to Mass at a picture-postcard, white-frame Episcopal church. As we feared, it's a made-up jumble of new-agey language and ceremony, seemingly invented only yesterday. We come away annoyed and grieving at the way the Episcopal church – *our* church – has rejected traditional rites and gravitas and a sense of the sacred.

Later in the day, we visit a part of the island where seals congregate. It's a lovely, quiet, windswept place with the sun shining brightly on the water and rocky islets just offshore. The seals are farther away than I'd hoped, but they're still fairly visible. Still more distant are shapes that may be sea lions. While strolling through a small forest nearby, we come upon one of nature's great treats, a pileated woodpecker – strange, outsized with a brilliant red head.

The writer Karen Armstrong finds God to be "an ineffable, unknowable, indescribable presence" that is experienced in music, poetry, nature, sex, and love. Not always, but as often, it seems, as in intentional worship.

CHAPTER TWENTY-TWO
HARD ROAD TO THE HUKILAU

Even on the island with plenty of leisure, we still didn't get around to mastering the tent. We joked that we might be starting a new trend in travel: drive around in a classic VW camper and stay in motels. There is already a similar fusion known as glamping. The website www.glamping.com defines it as "where stunning nature meets modern luxury." Also – this made us feel more up to date than embarrassed – "It's much more than a nice tent." The same can be said for a Hampton Inn. On the other hand, glamping sites offer "their own unique advantages. You can wake up in a yurt on a mountaintop" or "reside in the forest canopy in a treehouse." A Best Western can't match that. We considered a few opportunities to glamp but rejected them as too expensive.

From Lopez, it's back across the Columbia River and down the Oregon coast. Driving along on the Washington side, a sign for a ferry appears. Why not? We drive over a little bridge onto an island and follow a winding road for half an hour or so, hurrying to make the once-an-hour crossing. At the landing, the one person working on deck is casting off the stern lines. When she sees us, she puts the ramp back down and waits and smiles broadly. She's a VW nut. She has owned three vans herself, one of which dropped its engine in the road *while she was driving.*

We're skeptical, but not for a minute do we think about challenging her. We've been in the game long enough to know the rules of discourse; old-VW nuts tend to embellish their stories. We talk vans all the way across the river. We drive off into Oregon feeling good about once again having had another chance encounter that felt like running into an old friend.

It brings to mind a book a New York City neighbor had great success with – *Instant Intimacy*. He told me about it one evening over a beer. Said he'd made $50,000 from it in the short time it took him to fly from Chicago to New York after being on the Oprah show. Without reading it, I knew I had a file cabinet full of unpublished work that was better than his little book. He wasn't even a writer. He was a psychologist, and the best I could tell, all he did was walk his dogs and sit around looking at our beautiful neighbor when now and then she stood naked in her window. I never saw her once. I didn't like the guy. I can only guess that the book appealed because of the universality of the kind of experience Ann and I have just enjoyed on the ferry and in Portland and to a lesser extent in gas stations and parking lots and at stop lights all over the west. I admit grudgingly that if he did even a halfway decent job of describing the mystery of that, he deserved to make some money.

Along the Oregon coast, highway 101 is famous for its Pacific vistas. They are spectacular even in sheeting rain and high wind and even when we're caught in what seems to be a funeral procession of RVs. We can hardly focus on the views, though, for thinking about having to put up the tent at the end of the day. I've made reservations at a KOA on the outskirts of the town of Waldrop, and we're determined to use the thing no matter how hard it rains. But, along the way, Ann handily comes up with an idea about how we could still "camp" by stowing our gear in the van's nooks and crannies and on the front seat, sleep in the van, not put up the tent, and avoid getting wet, chilled, and dispirited.

As we turn into the KOA, she is chanting priest-like the litany of pleasures that await us when we're sleeping in the van and the rain is pounding on the roof and the wind is howling. I interrupt her to note that spending the night squeezed between two gargantuan Winnebagos, which is where we would be, doesn't seem much like "camping," and furthermore there are "lodges" available at the facility. We can bicker with the most accomplished of married couples, but not this time.

We're in luck. There's a vacancy. Several, in fact.

Do I want a First- or a Second-Tier Lodge? I opt for First since it has a view of the water, even though it's raining so hard we won't be able to see it. Unfortunately, our original reservation is for two nights, and the Tier One Lodge is available only for the second. So, Tier Two it is.

It's a small, square cell lined with knotty pine in a structure that resembles a Quonset hut with faux log siding. It has a double bed on which is a suggestion of a mattress. No sheets or pillowcases. I could go out in the rain and dig out our sleeping bags from the rooftop luggage carrier, but I don't have that much adventure in me at the moment. No bathroom either, so the night would include trips across the so-called campground in the rain to the communal toilets.

I go back to the registration desk to negotiate. How about we stay in a Tier Two the first night, and move to a Tier One the next night? (Or check out and head for the nearest Hampton Inn, if the rain hasn't stopped by then.) I assume that since Tier One comes at a higher price it will have a bathroom. It doesn't. I say we'll stick with Tier Two and save the money. I mention what a nuisance it is to have an aged prostate and ask if I can borrow an umbrella.

That prompts the clerk to reveal that a Deluxe Cabin is available, and it does have a bathroom. I suppose when I first presented myself, she hadn't seen me as Deluxe Cabin material.

Besides having a bathroom (airplane size), the Deluxe Cabin has a tiny microwave and tiny fridge and tiny tv – in all, just right for travelling Hobbits. Also, instead of faux log siding like the Tier Two hut, it has cedar shakes.

The cabin, Deluxe though it is, does not come with sheets, blankets, or towels. Chesterton would have thought it an adventure, though surely only a modest one.

Hard rain continues all night and through the following day, so we stay put in the Deluxe Cabin. Ann has more work than usual, and I soldier on at my blog. To that extent, it's like most days – the two of us in a small space making letters appear on our computer screens. But on this day, the space is smaller than usual, and the light is bad, and there are no chairs. We sit in the double bed shoulder to shoulder backs against the wall cushioned by a single pillow. We subsist on peanut butter, crackers, and water, which I go out in the rain to dig out of the van.

At supper time, we ignore the rain and drive into town to dine at the Flounder Inn, a restaurant I've found on the internet. Ann will go hungry before she'll eat flesh of any sort, but she can usually find something acceptable at any restaurant. I'm more flexible, and I'm sort of hoping I'll be forced to have flounder.

As it happens, the Flounder Inn is actually a rough bar, and it's out of flounder. While we study the menu, Ann has a seltzer, and I have a Jim Beam, the best bourbon available. I choke down some fried clams, before we give up. I go to the bar to pay the $8.34 check. I ask the bartender/cashier to go over the young waiter's arithmetic, and he gets huffy. It takes a while for me to make him understand that I think the charge is too low, not too high.

Next day, not far down the highway, we stop in the little town of Yachats for a late breakfast. The café is a cool place like you might find near a university. We enjoy bagels with some kind of tofu spread and get a couple of vegan bearclaws with marionberries for the road. We leave feeling restored and make our way to the next small town, Florence. There, having endured two nights in the KOA Deluxe Cabin – I can't remember why we had stayed the second night, but I assume there was a real good reason, such as doing serious penance – we give ourselves a treat, a nice A-frame cottage at the edge of town out near the famous Oregon dunes.

The cottage beats the KOA Deluxe Cabin, but it's not the borderline-luxurious change it appeared to be in photos on the web. When we open the door, a strong smell of fried fish whooshes out as if it's under pressure. It's missing some light bulbs. The furniture is dirty, and the upholstery is threadbare. A major selling point, the patio, turns out to be a stone's throw from the highway - literally. I throw a couple when the traffic lets up, and they land near the yellow line in the middle.

After a while, the proprietor/manager, a middle-aged woman, knocks on the door. She looks as tired as the cottage. I think of the bedraggled motel-owning widow at the beginning of *Tender Mercies*. The woman in Florence carries a large plastic tub of pots, pans, and silverware. I suppose she had taken them somewhere for washing.

The string of disappointments that is threatening to make us think ill of Oregon ends the next day. When Ann finishes her work in mid-afternoon, the sun is shining, and we drive to nearby Honeyman State Park. Hardly anyone is there. It has trails in wooded areas around a lake and at the western end, the dunes. Even low dunes like the kind bordering some beaches can be difficult to climb. These Oregon dunes are high. Partway up, I begin hearing the music from *Lawrence of Arabia,* but I stay with it and try not to think about how much easier Ann is finding the effort than I am. I'm determined to get to the top; I have some Keats I want to recite.

"Or like stout Cortez when with eagle eyes
He stared at the Pacific – and all his men
Look'd at each other with a wild surmise –
Silent upon a peak in Darien."

I am on a peak by the Pacific, but I don't get to be Cortez; there are more dunes beyond the one I have just conquered, so the sea is not visible. No telling how many I'd have to climb, if I'm going to stare in wild surmise at the Pacific. More positively, I record that we do not encounter any ATVs or dune buggies.

The day before, while cruising down the main street of Florence, population 8947, Ann spotted a restaurant named Hukilau, as in the song she and countless other children sang. Even now, Ann periodically renders a verse or two of it complete with little dance steps to represent charming wonders, such as "we throw our nets out into the sea." (She performs the "Iowa Corn Song" well, too.) Of course, we have a meal at the Hukilau. A very good meal. An Asian fusion version of tofu curry and veggie tacos.

As we are leaving, the owner/chef comes out from his little kitchen to talk about the van. He has a Hawaiian father and a Japanese mother. He studied cooking somewhere. I think he said France. We talk amiably, energetically, and, as usual in van talk, without the normal reservations between strangers. It makes me wonder who I would be if I had always owned a classic VW van.

CHAPTER TWENTY-THREE
BEAR CAMP AND REDWOODS

The recommended route from Florence to Valley of the Rogue State Park near Grants Pass where we have a reserved a campsite is not to my liking. It goes way south on 101 to Crescent City, California, then back northeast for eighty-two miles on U.S. 199. The tattered Rand McNally wedged behind the driver's seat shows a direct route; just make a left at Gold Beach and go pretty much due east. Shorter is better; it's already midday, and we want to make camp in daylight. The road snakes through the Klamath Mountains, but the elevations shown on the map seem manageable.

The road doesn't have a number, and at one point, there is a gap. To me, these novel features are less important than the dotted line indicating that the route is scenic. Not to Ann.

In the ensuing discussion, she thinks she hears me say she lacks a sense of adventure. I'm pretty sure I didn't; I require a compelling reason to start a fight. Whatever I said, she countered – in a fairly loud voice – that one of us has to show good sense to preserve us from major inconveniences, in the circumstances, perhaps death. Finally, though, she agrees to try the short route.

In Gold Beach, I can't find the turnoff to Grants Pass, so I stop in a gas station and ask directions from a man in a worn truck. Before answering, he looks the van over as if it's a horse he might want to buy. "The road to Grants Pass?" He pauses. "It's the last turn before the bridge." He gives me an odd look, which I interpret as envy that we are off to have so much fun in that fine vehicle.

The turn was easy to miss. There is only a small sign: "Agness, 35 miles." On the map, this peculiarly spelled place looks to be about halfway to Grants Pass. (Nor does it escape me that "Grants Pass" probably needs an apostrophe.)

That first segment is a two-lane paved highway, and we encounter only a handful of other cars, but it still takes about an hour to drive the thirty-five miles. There are so many sharp twists and turns, I drive almost as much in second gear as in fourth. It's littered with rocks and blowdown. Along one side, the Rogue River is beautiful, but for much of the way the land between the road and the river is strewn with shabby RV and trailer parks. Not "scenic" in quite the way I expected. To Ann's credit, she doesn't say "I told you this was a bad idea," but I can tell she's thinking it.

A few miles shy of Agness is a turnoff to someplace called Bear Camp. It isn't on the map. A large sign warns that the road is closed in winter. We keep going.

After a while, we come to the municipal limits sign. There is little else to indicate that it's much of a town – mostly just a utility line now and then leading into dense forest where I suppose there are houses. And then the road ends. A barricade with a large stop sign stretches across the right of way.

Next to it is a one-room frame building with peeling paint, a cliché of a country store. Out front, two men are sitting on broken-down lawn chairs, drinking beer, and taking it easy in a big way. One has a white beard that hangs down over the bib of his overalls. They give the impression that they might have been there a long time. Maybe they are props to make the scene look fully rustic. Maybe they aren't real; maybe I'm imagining them.

"I'm looking for the road to Grants Pass," I say.

That starts a backwoods colloquy in which they have fun with the city people in the Volkswagen camper.

"You passed the turn about five miles back." They give each other the side eye.

"The one to Bear Camp?"

"Yep." That sets them to grinning.

"It goes to Grants Pass?"

"Yep." That pushes them to half giggling.

I keep entertaining them with questions and eventually learn that the road is not paved. And one lane. With few turnouts. Switchbacks. Blind curves. It would take two or three hours to make those fifty or so miles. Much of it runs along a ridge that is something over 4000 feet.

"A lot of times people wear out their brakes going down." That is laugh-out-loud funny.

I'm pretty good at spotting when someone is ribbing me, so I'm skeptical. I don't care that Bear Camp Road is not exactly an interstate. It will be passable. Probably a lot of fun. Anyway, I had once driven across the trackless Iranian desert in a vehicle that was subject to breakdowns.

Ann disagrees. Strongly. The possibility of wearing out brakes has gotten her attention.

To give her a moment to gain perspective, I go into the store to get a snack. Except for beer and soda and a few bags of chips suspended from an overhead rope by clothespins, it has little to offer. When I come out, munching Fritos, Ann's position is unchanged.

Driving slowly back toward the turn to Bear Camp, she makes several points that despite my eagerness to embrace the adventure – such opportunities don't come along all that often – I agree with.

We lost cell phone connection miles back, and there is no reason to think it will return while we're feeling our way over the pass. How would we call AAA? A forty-eight-year-old Westie is not likely to travel on an unpaved road for long without breaking down. We have too little gas to allow for a wrong turn. According to the yahoos, we might be the only ones travelling that road. We could be in for a long walk in the dark in bear country. I drive past the Bear Camp turnoff without slowing.

We retreat to Gold Beach, defeated, and I phone the campground on the other side of the mountains to let them know we aren't going to make it. The nearest motel vacancy is in Crescent City, fifty miles farther south. It's clean and bear-free, but otherwise unlikely to quality for a Fodor recommendation.

Before going to sleep, I read up on the road not taken. I learn that some people died on Bear Camp Road when they got caught in a snowstorm. I find no mention of anyone dying in good weather, and snow has not started yet. We could have made it. Maybe. Maybe not, though.

The lady on the motel desk warns that even the recommended route to Grants Pass, which runs northeast from Crescent City, is perilous. She should know. She drives those eighty-three miles once a month to shop at Costco. "Don't try it at night," she says one hand raised, index finger extended to emphasize the point. "And it's very windy. Also, give yourself plenty of time."

I enjoy a hearty breakfast of a Honey Bun microwaved to perfection in its cellophane wrapper. I remind Ann that breakfast is the most important meal of the day, but she skips it and gets right to work. In solidarity, I sit on the bed and draft a blog post. At checkout time, she still hasn't finished, so I, always willing to do my part, drive her to a Starbucks to continue her work there.

While waiting, I get some maps from the local National Parks Office and learn a bit about visiting the redwoods, which we are about to enter. I find a campground in Del Norte Coast Redwoods State Park just seven miles farther down 101. The campground doesn't take reservations, so I drive out, claim a site, and pin my permit on the marker.

When Ann finishes, we have a late lunch at a Mexican restaurant and go to a grocery store for provisions. There is still about an hour of daylight left when we pull up to the site, but as usual it seems like a lot of trouble to put up the tent. The surface is part hard-packed earth, part gravel, and anyway we're only going to be there overnight. We take gear out of the inside and stuff it into the cargo carrier on top to keep it dry and sleep in the van.

The "bed" in the van is narrow. It encourages intimacy like a mother cat has with a litter of kittens, which is pretty nice if you're a kitten, less so if you are an aged human. Still, we're asleep by eight, feeling a sense of victory. We are not in a motel; we are *camping*.

As I whiled away the previous afternoon waiting for Ann to finish her work, I thought about ways to have better road trips in the future. Most important, Ann would take some time off. Then, if we should finally make peace with the tent, we would put it up only if we were planning to stay in one place for several days. We would reserve campsites months in advance. Drive short distances each day. In general, do whatever was necessary to call forth the free-spirited selves without which the classic VW camper was just a vehicle.

Next morning, we break the seals on the box containing the camp stove and make coffee. We get back on 101 and stop for two short hikes along the way. We are too eager to get to Humboldt State Park in the heart of the redwoods to do more. Before leaving Austin, we tried to reserve a campsite in or near the park, but none were available. The best we could manage was a VRBO house in Eureka, "the principal city of the Redwoods Empire." Seeing the redwoods from a city doesn't seem right, but it turns out OK.

From there, we drive fifty miles to Avenue of the Giants and enjoy a walk near its north end. We find the trees every bit as impressive as they are said to be. When we finish, it's the middle of the afternoon. We had planned to go to the Grove of Titans also, but we've seen enough redwoods. We get back on busy 101 and return to Eureka.

Along about this time, we begin considering the route back to Texas. In a way we are only dimly aware of, if at all, we're thinking about more than just the best route. The adventure urge is beginning to wane, and dancing ineffably around the edges of our consciousness is reflection on what the hot urge to have fun has come to and who we're going to be after it's over. We know the answer, but we've not quite owned up to it and said it out loud.

CHAPTER TWENTY-FOUR
MECHANICS

In Marin County, north of San Francisco, we visit old friends, the Fooses. At UT, Dean and I were suite mates at the Christian Faith and Life Community, an ecumenical institution that offered lectures, seminars, and worship services. It was so academically demanding, it was like attending two colleges at once. I lasted one semester; Dean, longer. After college, he attended Princeton Theological Seminary and became a Presbyterian minister. I should have asked him to bless the van before leaving to go north to Tahoe.

While we're with the Fooses, a headlight goes out. Old-van parts, even headlights, are hard to find, so I'm relieved to find a nearby garage called Auto Haus that specializes in German cars, including old VWs. I'm waiting in the driveway when the proprietor arrives.

"I only work on *water-cooled* VWs," he says. We're standing next to one. Its headlights look just like the ones on my air-cooled van. To my untrained thinking, the connection between cooling system and lights is difficult to understand. For a moment, I consider telling him it would be our secret if he'd make an exception in my case, but I settle for asking him if he knows anyplace where I can get a new old light. He suggests an outfit thirteen miles north in Novato.

A guy on the phone says, "Come on up." We say goodbye to the Fooses and go. Ann works during the drive, and after we get there, she continues at a table in a Whole Foods Market.

It's Friday, and when I arrive at the shop around 10:30, the owner, who is the sole mechanic, is about to close and enjoy a long weekend. Since I only need a headlight, he had waited for me. I like him more than the guy at Auto Haus. He is wowed by the van. He circles it a couple of times, murmuring a mechanic's version of sweet nothings, then gets down to business.

"I think we've got some lights like that." He does. He has a lot of lights like that – a couple of large boxes full salvaged from VWs gone to their junkyard rest never to overheat again. He picks through the pile, holds one up, and pronounces it acceptable. I'm relieved.

What he says next surprises me.

"Wouldn't you rather have a new sealed-beam type? You can see a lot better with them."

I guess he thought I might be a purist who would want original equipment. I'm not. I buy two of the new improved kind, and one thing leads to another, and before he finishes, his long weekend has shrunk to ordinary size.

He starts by showing me how to fix a taillight I didn't known was out. The first step is to check the fuse. Tom had taught me that and had given me some extra fuses for the road. The fuse box is hard to get at, hard even to see, but my man in Novato, Chris, is undaunted. He twists himself in a knot under the steering wheel, reaches up into the recesses behind the dashboard, finds the right fuse in the panel, pulls it out, checks it, and finds it working. His second move is easier. He takes the lens off the light, removes the bulb, and scratches the contact point on the driveway. That's all it needs. I have a screwdriver. I can do that if I need to.

He saws off and puts rubber caps on two sharp-pointed machine screws on the inside of the door that raises up over the engine compartment – the screws I've cut my head on several times. Chris may have noticed the oversized Band-Aid on my head. Good man, that Chris. Not quite in the angel category like Cindy, but good.

He applies some stuff to the rubber trim around the back window to keep it from deteriorating further.

We talk paint and wax, and I tell him I fear a new paint job is in my future; the Turtle Wax Ann and I applied on Lopez Island was not as effective as I had hoped. He applies a German wax to a spot, and I'm impressed. I buy two containers of it.

We talk overheating. Chris recommends keeping the temperature under 180. I don't like hearing that. We've already been driving slower than I want, and the temp is often higher than 180. I follow his rule for a few days, then arbitrarily settle on 210 as the limit. So far, I haven't burned up the engine.

Chris offers to change the oil, if I'll give him some time. I go to Whole Foods where Ann is just finishing her work. We have lunch, and afterward, she takes a walk while I go back to the shop.

More repairs and more schooling. Chris adjusts the valves and the brakes, including even the hand brake. He makes sure the tires have proper pressure. Like Tom, he recommends using only high-octane gas and a zinc-containing oil. I buy a couple of liters for the road. Also, a T shirt with a VW bug printed on the front. It's a nice companion piece for the two with a red van that we picked up in the yuppie pizza bar in Hood River. Some travelers collect coffee cups or decorative plates.

When Chris is finished, I tip him a bottle of Jack Daniels. We drive away at 3:30 and point the tip-top-shape, classic Westfalia toward Lake Tahoe. We don't get far, though, before we are held up by a wreck.

It clears in an hour or so, and Ann takes the wheel. She drives us the rest of the way, which includes Donner Pass in the dark. The 7239-foot summit is doable even for an old VW by staying in the truck lane and going slow. Nonetheless, it's challenging. The ascent covers forty miles, and the descent on the east side has a 5% grade for most of five miles, and then another 5% grade a little farther on. The course we have chosen takes us through Truckee at the north end of the lake, and that makes the drive still more arduous. We have a reservation in South Lake Tahoe, forty-seven miles down a two-lane highway, which seems to have more sharp curves and switchbacks than straightaways.

We stay two days, do some walking, and wonder why we've come. In Tahoe, people enjoy winter and summer sports, but we're there between seasons. The picturesque lake is choppy and whitecapping, and when we try to take a walk along the shore, a cold wind sends us back inside. We could gamble, but driving the van across country is all the gambling we have in us. We drive away from the hotel eager to get to Reno, where we'll turn south and enjoy a few days along the east slope of the Sierras.

As we pull into the parking lot of a nearby supermarket for breakfast and road snacks, the oil warning light comes on. To the extent the old van's braking system allows, I screech to a stop. I hurry around to check the dipstick and find a growing pool of oil on the pavement. It's coming out of the filter, which apparently was not attached properly. Chris immediately drops from near-angel status to careless mechanic. I tighten the filter with my hand, and the flow lessens and finally stops. I persuade myself that I've fixed the problem, though the size of the spill would have told an objective observer that the engine had given its all and had no more oil to leak. Nevertheless, I start pouring in the expensive German oil Chris has sold me. It takes a lot to make the dipstick reading what it should be. I ask Ann to start the engine while I watch. Until then, I had not known that motor oil could run through an engine with such speed. I might as well have poured it directly on the pavement.

I Google repair shops in the vicinity and make some calls and try not to think about how this adventure is coming to resemble my experience with a 1932 Studebaker that was always breaking down and no one knew how to work on. And oh yeah, there was that old motorcycle on which I spent too many hot summer hours jumping on the kick starter. And the Chevrolet with the perverse electrical system in Baghdad. Am I to be indelibly defined by entering voluntarily into relationships with unreliable vehicles?

Surprisingly, there are two garages close by that could get us going again, but they are booked for several days ahead. One suggests a shop in Reno with the unlikely name of Fibercraft. I'm skeptical, but I phone anyway.

A woman who sounds like someone's grandmother answers. I describe the problem, and she asks questions and conducts a shouting dialog with Adam, the mechanic, who is in the back of the garage on a crawler. After several minutes of this, she says, "Yeah, bring it in."

While waiting for the AAA wrecker, I try to think of some way to clean up the oil I have deposited on the Safeway parking lot. Unable to come up with anything less radical than calling ServPro, I consider pushing the van back over it, so it won't be so noticeable. We have stopped on an incline though, and the slick has oozed out into a crossing lane. I can't put the disabled van there. Fortunately, we're at the edge of the parking lot, and the store has just opened, so nobody drives through the pool, and I escape being socked in the nose by some proud owner of a new Corvette.

I look in the store for absorbent like garages use, but they don't carry it. When the wrecker comes into view, I tell an employee that there is an oil spill in the parking lot. We are pulling out of the parking lot before anyone in Safeway comes out. No one pursues us on the fifty-mile journey to Reno. So, we come out of incident with no more than a feeling of guilt. It was pretty strong, though.

We pull up in front of Fibrecraft at a little after three. Adam – boyish, round, and short – comes out to the street when he sees the wrecker. He's excited. Admiring. Pleased to get to work on our baby. Predictably, he says, "Come in the back and let me show you mine."

He has the van running properly by close of business.

We get a room in a casino close by the shop and enjoy champagne and a celebratory dinner.

Sitting in the Safeway parking lot ten hours earlier, waiting for the tow truck – Ann beavering away on a couple of rush requests, I with oil up to my elbows and fearing I might be attacked by an angry motorist or Safeway management – neither of us imagined such a happy ending. The day had gone from ordinary to near despair to relief bordering on elation. It reminds us of other up-and-down days on the trip. Trying as they were, they all ended well, but they are beginning to be wearing.

Maybe it's time to end to the adventure. Unlike classic quests and voyages, we can do that whenever we want. We don't have to wait until we've found the grail or achieved enlightenment. We can just end it. Go home by the most direct route and start a post-adventure life.

Not just yet though.

Scenic Highway 395 along the east slope of the Sierra Nevada lies ahead

CHAPTER TWENTY-FIVE
HIGH, LOW, AND IN BETWEEN

I'm relieved to find no oil leaking onto the pavement when I check the next morning, but I keep an eye on the warning light for much of the day.

The Sierras lie to the west of Route 395, and a flat, arid, valley to the east. The highway is winding, but pleasantly winding, not scary winding. There are points of high elevation, but the van takes them without a problem. Little by little, driving this beautiful road without mishap, our adventure spirit returns. And it gets a big boost from a couple of days in Mammoth Lakes.

We are especially energized by some hiking at fairly high altitude. The first day we cover about two miles around Horseshoe Lake. The trail is flat, but the elevation is nine thousand feet, which can be taxing. I manage it without even much huffing and puffing. The next day, we hike 4.5 miles to Rainbow Falls. The trail has plenty of up and down, and it peaks at a little over nine thousand feet. Nine months earlier, I was in severe, almost constant back pain. I come down from Rainbow Falls thinking about walking the Camino de Santiago de Compostela one of these days. Not the whole five hundred miles; I don't feel that good. But maybe two or three weeks of it.

The van performs as well as I do. We take a picture of it at Minaret Peak in front of a sign that reads "Elevation 9256 feet."

On down 395 is the town of Lone Pine, population 2035. Between it and Mt. Whitney, California's highest peak, are the Alabama Hills, 25,000 acres of which is overseen by the Bureau of Land Management. Barren, rocky, arid, it looks like the perfect setting for a Western movie, which in fact it has been many times. Starting with a Fatty Arbuckle silent film in 1920 and continuing until the 1970s, some 400 were made there. Some nonwesterns too, including *The Charge of the Light Brigade, Jonathan Livingston Seagull,* and *Kim.* The site has markers where well-known scenes were filmed. We spend the day walking around with the ghosts of Gene and Dale, Peck, Eastwood, Bogie, and other Hollywood legends. In town, a museum displays artifacts and recounts filming stories.

We had never heard of Lone Pine until we stumbled across it on the internet sometime after leaving Reno. That was surprising. Ann has a degree plus a year or so of graduate study in film history. In college, she would watch as many as three movies a day, and she has a special interest in westerns. To visit Lone Pine is a delight.

Lone Pine stands out in another way, too. There we stay in the crummiest motel of the entire trip. It is the little town's only available room that night, so I suppose I should be grateful, and I am – but only a little. Sleeping in the van on the shoulder of the highway would have more been more comfortable, but we didn't know that until we'd checked in and unloaded.

It has one bed, a queen that is only inches from the wall on one side. And there is too little space on the opposite side to allow moving it away from the wall. We are grateful that it has clean sheets, since it seems it would be impossible to change them. I'm tempted to stick around the next morning to see how it's done.

When checking in, I notice a sign instructing guests to come to the desk if they want ice. I do that. No one is at the desk, but on the counter is a classic bell like those used to summon bell boys in old hotels. I push the little plunger down and wait. After a bit, the proprietress emerges from a back room. She's another bedraggled, beaten-down looking woman like the one who ran the seedy A-frame in Oregon. I hand her my bucket, and she goes outside. I tag along. She enters her apartment and reaches into her personal fridge and gets me a handful of cubes.

The television screen is tiny, and reception is blinky. It's Friday, when we like to watch *PBS Newshour* with Shields and Brooks followed by *Washington Week*. PBS is not on offer. But it doesn't matter much. Ann is using her hotspot to access the internet and is fully engrossed in New York real estate ads. After she becomes discouraged by prices, we try to watch something on Netflix. A soothing *Father Brown* episode would have done nicely. We've turned to the amiable priest often of late. But the internet connection is too intermittent to enjoy it.

As we're going to sleep, Ann says, "I'm ready to end this trip." I'm glad to hear it; so am I.

We continue south toward the left turn that will take us onto I-40 and the Mojave Desert and much of the way back to Austin.

Along the way, we happen onto another film-related moment when we cross the aqueduct that caused the Jack Nicholson character in *China Town* that trouble with his nose. It's near a mostly dry lake that is said to be the premier source of dust in the United States. No movie reference there, just something curious. You just never know what you're going to run into when you take a long drive.

After a night in the town of Ridgecrest at a motel near a forbidding fence around the Naval Air Weapons Station – hadn't expected that either, since it's a long way to the nearest naval vessel – we get on I-40 and joust with legions of tractor-trailer rigs bullying their way across the Mojave. They rumble past us making a hell of a noise, and they seem to take pleasure in changing lanes with as little distance between us as possible. Maybe I imagine the part about them taking pleasure, like a sort of grumpy traffic mirage.

The Harleys are another matter. The in-your-face thunder of modified pipes and the show-off lean when they swerve in front is unmistakably political. It says, "we bearded bad-asses are as important as you wimpy elites." They make a good point, but I don't like the way they're making it.

The semis and hogs make us feel like intruders on their private road. It's annoying, and the feeling is amplified by their damn noise. We're making too much of it ourselves.

The van's powerful replacement engine is loud. So is the wind whipping through open windows. (The expensive after-market air conditioning system contributes to engine overheating, so we can't use it.) So, listening to the radio or CDs is futile. We could use ear phones and blue-tooth transmission from some sort of gadget, I suppose, but that has never occurred to us. Too old, I guess. Anyway, now that I think about it, such a high-tech fix strikes me as improper. Listening in the isolated zombie state induced by earphones while traveling in the together spirit of a VW camper just won't do.

Besides, if we could listen to the radio, we would probably be drawn to the political drama of our times. That's what happens in our Prius. Happily, the van forces us to take a break from it. Much of the time, we can't even get an internet signal to check on events via phone. We're a rolling oxymoron – cut off from the world while being cuffed around by the über-worldly noise of the internal combustion engine.

To the side of the highway, there is little to see other than sandy soil and a scattering of low plants (mostly sagebrush, I think). We're surprised to read on a poster at a rest stop that the desert is home to bobcats, mountain lions, rattlesnakes, rabbits, tortoises, and other creatures. It isn't as empty as it looks. Not as quiet either.

Standing beside the van with the engine off and, at intervals, with no passing traffic, we still have to contend with the sound of desert wind. It whistles and hums seemingly without interruption. It's not loud, but my hearing aids amplify it to the point that normal conversation requires some head twisting in search of a good angle.

Improbably, the day's noise engenders a certain stillness. After straining for a while to converse, we abandon the effort and occupy ourselves with studying the desert, noting a slight variation here, a bit of color there, thinking our own thoughts, and slipping into the restorative calm of companionable silence.

Late in the day, the highway climbs out of the desert, and we enter a familiar world – one with people, variation, and water.

Off and on, close by the Interstate, historic Route 66, the Depression corridor of Okie hope, has been preserved. It is, however, more kitschy theme park than museum, including even faux Burma Shave signs. In Arizona, the Grand Canyon takes a star turn. Many roads lead there. Want to raft it? Information half a mile ahead. See it by helicopter? Turn right for the booking office. Some day, perhaps, but now, we're headed for the barn.

In the evening, we settle into a motel in the town of Kingman and return to observing the televised presentation of American democracy being tested. It's an unsettling state of affairs, and my thoughts turn to something I've been reading about recently, the third-century religious hermits who retreated to the Egyptian desert in search of peace. I don't know if they found it, but I expect they did. Our morning in the Mojave showed us that deserts can do that to some extent even in the presence of motorcycles and trucks.

CHAPTER TWENTY-SIX
GOING HOME

The long ascent on the approach to Flagstaff is another contest with engine overheating. Even at 40-45 miles an hour, the temperature touches 220. We should take a cooling break or two, but we don't. Eagerness to cover the remaining miles makes us careless. We get away with it, though.

At seven thousand feet, Flagstaff is cool, and the air is clear. It's bordered by mountains and forests of sweet-smelling Ponderosa pine. It should engage us, but it doesn't. The motel window offers a view of the mountains, but in the foreground, I 40 dominates the picture. A short, easy hike on a trail called Fatman's Loop, gets me so winded, it registers as failure.

The blahs continue at the next stop, Gallup, New Mexico. We drive its substantial length on Business 40/Rt 66 to a La Quinta at the far end. My first impression is that the town is poverty stricken, lifeless, and ugly. I find no reason to revise my view after driving its length twice more in search of supper. We try three Mexican restaurants and leave each one without ordering. It's the least vegan/vegetarian-friendly town we encounter on the trip. It would not be a surprise to learn that even the guacamole is made with pork. We settle for a school-cafeteria-quality microwaveable supper from a supermarket, which we enter and exit under the watchful eye of a security guard. A door at the far end of a row of registers is locked, presumably as a precaution against theft.

In Santa Fe, our spirits are lifted by two days of sightseeing and a visit with old friends, the Ratliffs. It has been some years since we've been together, and it's a great pleasure to be with them. We go over old memories, calibrating recollections that have grown dim; we reflect on decisions made and courses taken and not taken and how we have come to be the people we are.

From Santa Fe, we drive for a day through flat, dry, country, much of it hot, and end with a night in Lubbock. The vast landscapes in that part of New Mexico are interesting, even enjoyable, in their way. Lubbock is not. Along with Midland, it embodies much that I deplore about the Texas way. In fact, though, neither city is likely to be as given to self-interest and as devoid of high culture as I imagine; I have little information about them.

The final long day takes us through cattle country, where it seems there is a law requiring pickup trucks to have bumper stickers in support of Trump and equating abortion with murder and opposing any limitations on gun ownership. It's a mournful country-song of a place as in the Mac Davis lyric "I knew I'd wind up in jail or dead if I have to stay."

* * * *

Back in Austin, I reflect on what we have done, how it came to be, and where it was leading.

A couple of years ago, we were enjoying a cocktail after a day of middle-class, home-owner ordinariness – inspecting the front-yard cedar elm for ball moss and wondering if the basement was going to take on water during the rain that was forecast and that sort of thing – when the idea of buying a classic van dropped in. We had considered it before, but this time the urge was not to be denied. Well, why not? Before the evening was over, we were shopping for one online.

For several months, we considered price, which was substantial if we were to avoid buying a project and risk turning into old-VW nuts, and how neither of us knows much about auto repair – pretty good reasons not to proceed. But it came down to this: Ann would say, "Let's have some – her voice rising in pitch and amplitude – FUN!" I would respond, "YES!" After intermittent repetition of this this jolly antiphon, we became so keen to have an Age-of-Aquarius relic, we bought the one we've just driven to Lopez Island, sight unseen, from a classic-car dealer in Chicago and had it shipped to us.

We spent the better part of a year driving it around town, getting used to lack of power steering, having repairs and improvements made, and growing a vision of a long road trip that was all blue skies and folk songs, feeling young and bold, and, somehow, something akin to fulfillment. It was ours for the asking. Just start the engine and go.

As it turned out, the trip presented some challenges (see above), but we muddled through. On balance, fun outweighed everything.

Mile after mile, there was the fun of sightseeing: spacious skies, purple mountains that are indeed majestic, amber waves of grain. Those delights alone made up for having to spend two nights in Lubbock.

It was fun to be envied by people who wished they had a van like ours and to watch memories of the summer of love light up their faces when they circled around the van in gas stations and parking lots all over the west. It was fun to climb in and magically turn back the calendar and become guest members of the counterculture. It was fun to be saluted by peace signs.

But as important as having fun was, it was a superficial part of what had motivated us. Underlying it was restlessness. I suppose most people have at least a touch of that in them; Ann and I have a lot. We can hardly resist (and why should we?) checking to see what's out there. It could be fun. And it might be more fulfilling than the life of now. It might even touch on disquieting questions about meaning.

A couple of weeks before my fiftieth birthday, I enrolled in law school, graduated, became a member of the New York Bar, and immediately "retired." That's the Bar's term; more to the point was Bartleby, the Scrivener's, phrase, "I prefer not to."

After two walk-throughs, we bought the ramshackle fourteen-bedroom monastery in the Adirondacks as a vacation home, spent nineteen years renovating it, lived in it as our primary residence for several years, sold it at a loss, and moved on to another way of being.

We tried to move back to New York City where we had happily lived off and on since 1989. But real estate prices had risen, and our means had shrunk, and we were not yet willing to live in the small space that would be all we could afford.

We moved back to Austin, purchased a centrally located, charming, 2458-square-foot house that was built in 1929, lived in it for just over a year, sold it, and rented a 1000-square-foot condo.

None of these explorations gave us quiet hearts – bits and pieces and occasional relief, but not the whole package. Unexpectedly, the van adventure did give us the antidote we had long sought – an unqualified understanding of who we are.

On the road, it came to us that New York City was more than a place where we had enjoyed living. It alone would give us what we had known as children in Muskogee and Port Arthur, where it felt inexplicably and indescribably right to be and where we were unconditionally happy to be who we were.

To be sure, much of what we love about New York exists to some extent in many cities. Great art museums, outstanding architecture, grand opera, classical music, renowned universities, world-class medical facilities, progressive politics, public transportation, shoulder-to-shoulder multiculturalism are not unique to New York City. But in New York City, they are realized in larger quantity and quite often in superior quality.

New York does, however, have an indefinable something that cannot be found anywhere else – the feel and smell and sounds encountered on the streets and the excitement and satisfaction of living in what is effectively the capital of the world.

To Ann and me, these features of New York City life are constant sources of joy and enrichment, but we *can* live reasonably happy, fulfilled lives without them, if necessary. We have done so in the past.

There is, however, one part of New York City we cannot gracefully accept living without: the ancient forms of worship combined with liberal Protestant ethics that is Anglo-Catholicism.

Anglo-Catholic churches exist in a few other American cities, notably Boston and Philadelphia, but in those other places, we would not enjoy the sustaining charm of living in New York. Not only that, we would be the new people in town, and we're at a time in our lives when we want to be at home. No place feels more like home than New York, particularly the Upper West Side of Manhattan.

None of this came to us as a sudden revelation while driving around the west; we had known for a long time that's who we are. What came to us on the road was the clear realization that it was essential.

CHAPTER TWENTY-SEVEN
TAKING CONTROL, LOSING CONTROL

We went to New York for a month during the Christmas holidays to shop for an apartment.

On December 17, we made an offer on one, then enjoyed a couple of weeks immersed in the special pleasures of New York Christmas. We returned to Austin in early January, and after a little haggling, we reached agreement with the seller. We went back to New York in February to be interviewed by the Coop Board. We were deemed worthy, and on March 16, we closed on the purchase.

That's a normal course for a New York residential real estate transaction, neither slower nor faster, and with the usual steps, but this outline omits the overarching presence of the pandemic.

Nor does it include my special preoccupation, fretting about the van. In imagining returning to live in the city again, we envisioned summer interludes messing about in New England like Frog and Mole in boats and occasional longer excursions into the Canadian Maritimes. And we would make those outings in the way we had not on the trip out west; Ann would take time off, and we would enjoy longer stays in one place and actually camp. First though, we would have to find someplace in the city to park the van. It was a problem that would bedevil us long after we were settled in. But we were unwilling to sell it; the journey had not yet run its course. It was a problem, but it was a relatively simple one. We would figure out a way.

Covid-19 was not simple. The pandemic raged throughout the period of our transition and beyond. At the time, there was no vaccine, cure was a sometime thing, deaths were increasing steadily. It also presented a variety of quotidian inconveniences for those who did not get sick.

****

The month at Christmas is as fully New York as we had hoped. It's as exciting as arrival and setting up residence was in 1988, when Ann began her legal career at the Wall Street firm, Cleary, Gottlieb, Steen, and Hamilton and when we moved back from London and Hong Kong. Once again, we are quickened by a sense of newness and possibility even as we feel like we have finally made it home.

The day after this most recent arrival, we attend Mass at St. Ignatius of Antioch. We are greeted like family members who have been too long gone, and at the same time as if it was only last Sunday that we were there.

We delight in night after night of classic Christmas music masterfully performed – the New York Philharmonic, the Chamber Music Society of Lincoln Center, the Gotham Early Music Society, Jazz at Lincoln Center with Wynton Marsalis, and more.

On a bus, en route to a program of songs performed by Ute Lemper, we fall into a favorite New York cliché. It's a fifteen-minute ride at most, but that is long enough to establish a relationship with a stranger. I still exchange emails with a man we met on the bus.

In hours of long walks, we renew acquaintance with the streets and buildings and smells and sounds of the Upper West Side.

But not everything that occurs during the month is to our liking. Midway in the period, I develop a gastrointestinal problem, but I keep it in check with Imodium and purposeful denial. Later, I add a cold, which quickly begins to seem like more than a cold, with a heavy cough and loss of voice, which comes on without the usual period of increasing hoarseness. Then, Ann develops a respiratory problem. We do our best not to cough on the plane back to Austin on January 7.

After a couple of weeks of treating symptoms, my cough abates. Ann's hangs on longer. In late January, she sees her doctor. He orders a chest x-ray and prescribes antibiotics and cough medicine. Around this time, news reports begin appearing about the Wuhan virus outbreak that began shortly before our holiday. In New York, we had stayed in a Columbia University apartment building for faculty and graduate students. At that season, many of the residents were presumably visiting relatives in Dubuque or Charleston. Those who were not away, spoke Chinese, and came and went with heaps of luggage like people carry on international trips. Had they been to affected areas of China, even Wuhan? Were they carriers?

Ann's doctor does not test her for Covid; at the time, few doctors were doing that. We never do get a test. But our symptoms are so similar to those of Covid, it seems likely that we had it. Despite my age, my doctors say all signs indicate that I'm younger than the birthdays indicate. Presumably that would include my immune system. Except for moderate hypertension and osteoporosis, Ann is in robust health. It's likely we would have had a less virulent case of Covid, if that was what we had.

By the time we close on the apartment purchase in March, the virus is widespread and lethal. New York City is especially hard hit. Hospitals are full, intensive-care units are in short supply, a hospital ship weighs anchor in the harbor, and there is not yet a vaccine. It is the pestilence that walks in darkness, the sickness that destroys at noonday that a Psalmist encourages the faithful not to fear. We do, though.

As we're driving through Arkansas en route to the closing, Mayor de Blasio declares a state of emergency, effectively closing the city. Too bad. We have committed, and we are on our way.

We had packed a futon, coffee pot, paint brushes, and drop cloths, so Ann can camp in the apartment and paint it while I drive back to Austin to vacate the condo and deal with the moving company. Somewhere between Memphis and Knoxville, we turn off I-40 to go to a supermarket and get provisions – beans, oatmeal, fruit, protein bars – to supplement what we have with us. We're too late. Panic buying is in full swing. Shopping carts are piled high with toilet paper. The parking lot is overflowing. We drive on.

As we listen to radio reports of how life in New York is being upended, we consider adjustments to our plan. With the city shut down, Ann will not be able to go out for meals, perhaps not even get anything delivered. In Harrisburg, Pennsylvania, where we spend the last night on the road, we find an REI store that is still open. Assuming she'll be able to buy some groceries in the city, we buy a bean pot and a skillet. And we begin thinking that I should stay with Ann, and we'll drive back to Austin together when she finishes painting.

Usually, the traffic around Newark airport, on the New Jersey Turnpike, and in the Lincoln Tunnel, is challenging. On this occasion, it's *Twilight* Zone absent. It feels like we are the only car in the tunnel. Manhattan streets are almost empty as we drive to a midtown hotel. Business is so bad, that for $170, we get a luxury suite about the size of our new apartment – two bedrooms, two bathrooms, and a pretty good-sized kitchen. After checking in, I find a grocery store that is letting people in a few at a time and buy microwave dinners.

In the morning, the business of becoming owners is conducted quickly and unceremoniously, starting with a brisk walk through deserted streets to the apartment for a final inspection before the ten o'clock closing. We are in and out so quickly, the seller's broker double parks.

The title company has suspended operations by then, but our attorney has persuaded the company to open up for our transaction since we were already halfway there en route from Texas. We ride an empty elevator to a high floor, where a receptionist is watching for us. She unlocks the door and lets us in, steps back, and points to a conference room. The woman who will run the closing is already seated at the far end of a conference table. Our lawyer is on one side; the seller's lawyer, on the other. The seller has signed remotely. Ann and I sit at the end opposite the closer. We all wear masks, and we apply hand sanitizer repeatedly. As instructed, each of us has brought our own pens. It would take an intrepid germ to cause harm amid all those precautions, but you never know.

The transaction feels like it's on life support. No small talk. The closing agent gives a perfunctory description of each document, slides them across the table one by one, and we sign by the stickies without reading them. It's over in minutes. We get the keys and start for the door with the closer and receptionist right behind us (but at a proper distance). They follow us out and lock the door. It feels like we are the only people in the building other than the security guard at the entrance. We probably are.

The handshakes and congratulatory wishes and sense of finality and new beginning that usually accompany residential closings has been absent, but we sort of make up for it by making a joyful noise on the way to get the car. We sing loud and clear, "Get your coat, and grab your hat. Leave your worries on the doorstep. Just direct your feet to the sunny side of the street." There is so little traffic our voices are about the only sound on the street. The handful of pedestrians who are out – most in scrubs or street cleaning uniforms – smile and give us thumbs up.

At the apartment building, we introduce ourselves to the doorman on duty, stash the contents of the car, enjoy an all-too-short look at our new home, and leave immediately for Austin, the original plan abandoned. For Ann to stay was risky, and she would be marooned there indefinitely, since moving in is prohibited by government order until Covid becomes less threatening. And when she had finished painting, traveling back to Texas by any means would be problematic.

We flee as if we are being pursued by a monster, which, in fact, we are.

As much as we have wanted to leave Austin, in the circumstances, it feels like safe harbor. In Texas, the incidence of Covid infections is smaller than New York's. And whatever problems we may face in Austin, we'll be better able to handle them. We know Austin intimately. We first arrived there right after high school, and we have lived there off and on for many years since. That history gives us everyday competence, a welcome attribute when facing a pandemic.

We cover the 1900 miles in a little over two days. We stop for gas only when the tank nears empty, and I wrap the pump handle with a paper towel when filling it. We drink little coffee and water so we can go long distances without bathroom breaks. We sustain ourselves mostly on power bars and peanut butter sandwiches. We do stop once at a Panera that is still serving. It has moved tables far apart and eliminated most wait staff. We don't linger. The motels are on automatic pilot. At a Hampton Inn, a clerk positioned well back from the desk pushes papers at us and slides key cards across the desk. The lobby is ghostly in the morning – no one working the desk, no guests, and for breakfast, a few paper bags each containing a bottle of water, a piece of fruit, and a cellophane-wrapped sweet roll.

Back in the Austin condo, we have drinks and fry the eggs that are about the only food on hand except for a couple of frozen hamburger buns, which we toast, and reflect on our situation.

We have become powerless. We can't affect the moving schedule or much else. Governor Cuomo and Mayor de Blasio will decide when we can move into the apartment we own. After they allow it, our building's management will make its own decision. The moving company will determine when they deliver to the city. Any number of people have a vote in our fate. We don't.

The condo lease expires at the end of April. Ann's work has dried up, so our financial situation is at the mercy of market forces, which themselves are at the mercy of the pandemic The comfort of having a drink or a meal and conversation with friends and family is a memory, and we or few others have yet turned to Zoom calls. You might expect that since no one has much control over anything, that would offer the comfort of solidarity. It doesn't; it increases our unease.

It's not the way we envisioned going home to New York City.

CHAPTER TWENTY-EIGHT
MARKING TIME

As we wait, we try not to feel too unsettled. It's difficult, though.

Walking in the park near the condo, Ann asks some young people to wear masks. They respond with, "Shut up, old lady." So much for the comfort of being back where we've come from. New York City has much higher rates of Covid infection than Austin, but in important ways it still seems less threatening. By and large, New Yorkers do not find consideration of the common good to be un-American; they are much more willing than Texans to wear masks and observe social distancing.

In the condo, which we leave as seldom as possible, we live surrounded by the clutter of the interrupted move. We packed books, dishes, and clothes before we lost control of the process. Boxes and goods still waiting to be packed are piled about us in every available space. We hope to see it all loaded onto the moving van immediately after the city and the coop allow move-ins, but whether the company will do that is not something they will tell me. They probably can't say. The moving business, like most, is in disarray. Orders are backed up, and the company has little more control over things than Ann and I do.

The condo lease will expire in a few weeks. Real estate activity of all sorts is on hold, so the landlord will probably be happy – relieved – to offer us a new lease, but I'm reluctant to do that. Surely, we'll be able to move before a year has passed. If we do, we'll be responsible for the entire one-year term. In the current situation, finding a new tenant to relieve us of our obligation is unlikely. I ask the landlord to extend the lease month by month, though I'm pretty sure he won't. His response earns him a place in the Good Landlords Hall of Fame. "Sure.

Whatever you want." I suppose his kindness is generated by his own pandemic situation. He lives in a suburb of New York City and has been working from home since the city shut down.

That takes care of one concern – a big one – but there are plenty of less important ones, and they keep coming.

I lose a hearing aid when I remove my mask, a common occurrence in these early days of mask wearing. The manufacturer will replace it (once), but the deductible is $300, and I'll be without it for a period of weeks. Not good. Constant "Huh?" is harmful to relationships, especially when two people are confined in a small space for twenty-two or twenty-three hours a day while dealing with wall-to-wall uncertainties. I'm sure I lost it in the car, so I poke around for a long time in the ten-year's accumulation of dirt and debris under the seats (it's better not to know what it's like down there), but I can't find it.

Ann takes a turn. In the process, she encounters a mystery. When both devices are placed close together on a table, they make a soft whistling sound as if they are singing to each other. Neither of us has ever heard one hearing aid alone make a sound. But as Ann scours the Prius, the lost aid does sing. "I'm here," it croons. "You're getting warmer. No, not that way. Now you're getting cold." With the aid of kitchen tongs, she plucks it from a crevice, and it goes quiet. Too fanciful? It does seem so. But that's what happened.

There is a smartphone app for the brand of hearing aid I have, and it has a locator function. I didn't know about it, though, and I'm glad I didn't. I prefer the mystery of a hearing aid singing solo.

I hope the hearing-aid mystery augurs a less onerous wait. It doesn't. The wait continues to be a slog. It reminds me of when my family relocated when I was a boy. Our goods were put on a Mayflower moving van in Toledo, and we drove the thirteen hundred miles to Beaumont. There we lived in a motel (a "kitchenette") for three months while my parents looked for a house. It was summer, so my brother and I were not in school. We were bored, we didn't have any friends, and we chose freely among the many ways to get into mischief that the situation offered. The level of stress Mother and Daddy felt must have been much the same as what Ann and I are going through. Covid was not a worry then, but polio was, and it was just as scary.

I turn to organizing and disposing of things in the storage unit that is stuffed with what we couldn't fit into the condo. Many of the boxes are vaguely labeled, so day after day I open them one by one to find out what's in them. We'll have no more room in New York than we do now, and for various reasons, using a storage facility there is impractical. I decide item by item what to keep and what to leave behind. It involves a fair amount of looking backward, like going through the worldly goods of a deceased loved one, but it's also about looking ahead. To some extent, each choice is a declaration of identity. Which doors shall we shut, which will we leave open? Who are we to be going forward? The question has more weight for people our age; do-overs are increasingly harder to come by.

I give away half our books. Maybe more. That's hard. From an early age, I was certain that having a large library was an indicator of status and merit, and I am reluctant to part with any. Reference and nonfiction titles are mostly keepers. Fiction is easier to let go of, since most novels and short stories can be replaced used at affordable prices, should the urge strike.

The four-volume text from a college world-lit course is an easy call, too. It has made every relocation since 1957. I reread favorite parts occasionally, but not often. Some bits, such as Montaigne and Erasmus, I've still not gotten to, but I will – one of these days. But if I never open any of the four volumes again, I still would not willingly part with them. They are souvenirs of a joyful adventure. I'm not going to leave them behind at this late stage.

There are a fair number of sentimental favorites. Some childhood books that turned up among my mother's things when she died, such as *Manners Can be Fun,* and *Val Rides the Oregon Trail.* High-school yearbooks, including those of my parents from the 1920s. A small collection of works on Muskogee and eastern Oklahoma.

I donate twenty or thirty books at a time to the Austin Public Library. After Covid restrictions cause it to close, I bless Goodwill Industries with hundreds, including 320 copies of my novella, *A Franklin Manor Christmas.* I wonder if someone who is shopping for used furniture or clothes will buy a copy, read about Professor Butch Regent's encounters with angels, and find something worthwhile in it?

The ten-quart Hobart mixer we bought at the nuns' moving sale goes to my son Murph who owns the bistro/bakery his mother and I started in 1981. Using the Hobart, Ann, a professional baker before going to law school, turned out heaps of bread, cookies, and assorted baked goods for the large parties and benefits we held at the monastery. Ann also parts with her commercial baking pans, cake circles, and other big-baking paraphernalia. Giving away these things amounts to a significant change of identity. It's acceptable, but not altogether welcome.

We find buyers for extra furniture, and that at least causes no goodbye pain. I make countless trips to the Goodwill store with donations of household items. The last thing to go is the ShopVac. I take it over immediately after locking the condo door the final time and depositing the keys in the property manager's lockbox.

We develop some health problems. They aren't serious, but we already have enough disagreeable stuff to deal with. An ankle injury from months earlier acts up and requires a couple of doctor's appointments and an MRI. I'm given a choice of surgery or immobilizing my ankle for a while with a boot. I decline both and rely on slowing down a little and anti-inflammatories. The condition eventually improves.

Ann has a bout with vertigo. She does Epley maneuvers while continuing her legal practice, demand for which is picking up. Like my ankle trouble, the vertigo goes away after a bit.

What to do with the van continues to be vexing. Taking it to New York as we move (whenever that is) will be impractical, so we decide to leave it in Austin and come back for it later, after I have searched out less unaffordable parking. But first I have to find a place in Austin to store it. I try a couple of self-storage units, but the vertical clearance in them is too low. I approach Tom and Roger to see if they will store it in their garage. As I expect, they don't have room, but Roger finds a place near their shop that has some shed-type facilities with high ceilings. For a modest fee, he will go over periodically and drive it a little. The place doesn't seem right, though. It's unpaved and dusty, and rodents are a notorious problem in vehicles that are stored for long periods in such conditions. An ordinary Texas hailstorm would batter the end that is partly exposed.

Eventually, I find a storage facility that meets our criteria. All I will have to do is disconnect the negative post on the battery, and it will be good to go when I come back for it. Disconnecting the battery is harder than it sounds, though; in the van, it's in a devilishly tight space. Instead of that, old friend Walle, who lives nearby, agrees to go by about once a month, start the engine, and let it run for a while. It's remarkably generous of him. The storage unit is only slightly wider than the van, so it's a tight squeeze to get into it. Walle is recovering from hip replacement and other problems. He is in chronic pain. At the time, I don't realize how severe it is, and I accept his gift gratefully and reflect on our sixty-plus year friendship.

So far, Ann and I are merely inconvenienced. Genuine suffering, though, is widespread and growing. This crisis is different from any the country has ever known. People cannot even touch each other, much less enjoy the comfort of an embrace. Nor do we have the succor of

Churchill's soaring eloquence or FDR's reassurance and governing skill or Lincoln's steady persistence or the brilliant cool Obama brought to bear during the financial collapse of 2008 or Bill Clinton's empathy.

As disheartening as the situation is, there is, at rare moments, a vague sense of community. Yo Yo Ma's *Songs of Comfort*, featured on the PBS Newshour, calls up Vera Lynn singing about the white cliffs of Dover. If you squint your eyes, self-isolation can be seen as sleeping in the Tube station during the Blitz, except for the obvious difference that our displacement is done alone or almost. While driving from New York, Ann and I listened to the Great Depression songs of Woody Guthrie. And imagining the new Depression that may well be on its way, we sang the Civil War song, *Hard Times Come Again No More*. As painful as those earlier trials were, they were made less unbearable by a sense of solidarity. We could sure use some of that now and the songs that go with it.

Even so, at our house, we're in good shape. Ann and I are in generally good health, we have plenty to eat, we take long walks, listen to music, sing, read, and wait with hope for the all-clear signal and better times.

CHAPTER TWENTY-NINE
MANHATTAN IN THE EARLY MONTHS OF COVID

On June 8, almost three months after closing on the purchase of the apartment, a moving van pulls up on 91st Street with our goods. Having to wait so long before being permitted to move in has been strange – surely moving in is included among the rights of ownership – but I don't dwell on it; almost everything is strange about this moment in history.

In the building, Covid precautions are mandatory. To get past the doorman requires using hand sanitizer from a wall-mounted container. Masks are required everywhere and always. Only two people are allowed in an elevator at the same time, and a single rider must agree before a second person is allowed on.

Outside the building, normal social exchanges are but a memory. Restaurants, museums, shops, and churches, including our own, are locked tight. This is not the New York we longed to return to, and it likely will remain in this odd state for a long time to come.

All that aside, it's remarkably quiet in the neighborhood, and that has a calming effect. The first night in the apartment, I am lulled to sleep by the building's thrum. It's like the sound and feeling aboard a ship. I suppose it's air conditioning units in neighbors' windows, but it's not hot enough yet for many to be running. I prefer to think the building is talking to me, wishing me sweet dreams and best wishes for our life here.

After the movers leave, Ann disinfects the apartment to the largest extent possible, giving special attention to anything anyone might have touched. We arrange for grocery delivery. We leave the apartment for a daily walk in the park but for little else.

As soon as it becomes possible, we get vaccinated, and after a period of months, mandatory restrictions and common-sense precautions become less intrusive. Then almost a year after moving in, it's possible to begin the renovation of the kitchen and bath that had to be postponed earlier. And now we feel little enough threat from Covid to move out until the work is finished. We use the enforced absence to rent a car and drive to Austin to get the van out of storage and enjoy a long holiday on the way back.

I handle important difficulties well enough, I think, but the little ones often threaten to be my undoing. In the year of living in Manhattan under Covid restraints, I have little fear of getting sick, but questions about the van often keep me awake at night. No matter how much I try to persuade myself to see van issues in proper perspective, I cannot, and we are so attached to the van, giving it up is unthinkable.

The starting point of my worries is simple. Where will we park it in New York? Covered park-and-lock garages with high clearance are uncommon, and the cost is upwards of $1000 a month. The least unaffordable ones are inconveniently located in one of the outer boroughs, and keeping it out there has the same amount of appeal for me as mandatory vaccination does for the MAGA crowd. Brooklyn/Bronx/Queens traffic is no place to drive an antique VW. After months of such worrying, I'm saved from complete insanity by our friends Vic and Pam offering to keep it in their barn. They are two hundred miles away in New Hampshire, but we anticipate taking it out for a spin only a few times a year. The cost of getting to the barn will be a lot less than parking in the city. And, as a bonus, we'll have reason to spend some time with our friends. It's a good solution, but it gives me something else to worry about.

How will I keep the battery charged over the winter? I could ask Vic to start it now and then, like Walle is doing, but he and Pam spend winters in Texas. If I show up in spring to find the battery dead, that will be a problem. On most cars, jump starting a dead battery is easy. Not the van. Its battery is larger than stock issue, and it fits so tightly in its compartment that attaching jumper cables or disconnecting the cables when it's stored is very difficult. I imagine a AAA guy being defeated. Even replacing the battery with a new one is hard. It's a silly worry really, but silly is my specialty. And I fail to recall the dead-battery remedy we used as teen agers – just push it and slip the clutch. Anyway, doing that on an isolated farm during a New England mud month is a problem of its own.

Meanwhile, I go to work on getting a New York Driver [*sic*] License. Oh boy. The New York rule is clear: "You must exchange your out-of-state driver license within 30 days of becoming a New York resident" or be treated as if driving without a license, which would be bad. Further, the exchange has to be done in-person at a DMV office.

That second requirement is a problem. DMV offices are closed on account of the pandemic. I write a letter. No answer. It doesn't matter, though. I'm not driving anyway. I'll get a New York license when Covid lets the DMV open again. Surely my failure to observe the thirty-day rule will be pardoned. I put it out of my mind. But not for long

When I try to register to vote, I learn that I must have a New York Driver License or a "REAL ID," which also requires a visit to the DMV. Fortunately, the DMV opens again before Covid-19 eats my franchise. I make an appointment and gather proofs of residence, age, and identity. Mask firmly in place, I wait outside the building on East 125th Street in Harlem for a long time on a summer day made hotter by heat radiating off pavement and buildings, and, as required, I don't show up more than fifteen minutes early. At the door, I present the official time-stamped, admission document. I am disappointed when the security guard hardly looks at it. I had been led to believe that every step in this process was seriously important.

At the window, my application is summarily rejected. The name on my Social Security card doesn't match exactly the name on my passport. My middle name is Joseph. It's the only middle name I've ever used – with one exception. When I applied for the card at age twelve, I wrote "Joe" in the blank for middle name. I thought it would be fun to be a "Joe." And that is what is says on the worn, seventy-year-old card that I stick through the slot in the postal glass that separates me from a clerk who has no more empathy than a Marine Corps drill instructor. Shaking his head, he tells me to go to the Social Security office and get a name change. He ends our brief encounter by shaking his head some more and saying he doesn't know how I got a Texas license in the first place. I turn away in shame.

Unlike the DMV, the Social Security office is still closed. I begin to worry so strenuously about not being allowed to vote, it overshadows worries about the van. There has never been a more important election.

Ann also has a driver license/Social Security card problem. She does not have the actual card in her possession. But it is her opinion as an Officer of the Court, a duly licensed member of the New York Bar, that according to the DMV website, presenting the actual card is not required to get a license. She argues her case to a clerk at the DMV. (She has no problem with taking on fool's errands.) He checks with a higher up before saying "the website is wrong." Due process, appeals procedures, those sorts of legal niceties have not yet found their way to the DMV.

Her situation is not so troublesome as mine, though. Because she needs merely a new Social Security card, not a name change like I do, the regulations permit doing it by mail. She fills out a form and sends it in along with her passport, and it works. I advise her to rough up the new card, sweat on it, and otherwise make it look suitably old, lest it appear to be counterfeit, and she finds herself turned away by DMV as I had been. She succeeds, though, and eventually, so do I. No teenager was ever prouder of their first license than we are.

With that, I can legally drive, but the van still has to be registered. I fill out a long, detailed form and drop it into a box at the DMV office in Harlem. I wait a long time for a response, but none comes. I reach someone in the state capital by phone. The VIN I had entered contained a typo. I express sincere regret and willingness to correct it forthright. She doesn't actually say, "Not so fast, Buster," but I hear it in her tone. Regulations require that corrections to applications be made online, and furthermore submitting an entirely new form with all information correct is not permitted. That was OK by me; filling out the form was tedious. However – this is the sticky wicket – for automobiles made before 1973 (the van is a '71), problem applications cannot be accessed online. I am sitting at my desk, thinking that maybe New York cars and I are a combination not meant to be, when the DMV opens again. I go back to Harlem and by God's mercy, I find a helpful clerk and straighten things out. On December 11. 2020, about six months after starting the process. I am handed license plates.

At this point, the only other requirement for driving the van legally in New York is an inspection. It's another seemingly simple task that actually is not, or so it seems for a while. Several years earlier, I had been told by a garage that inspections have to be made in the county of the owner's residence. That meant I would have to drive the van into Manhattan. As I have already made plain, I fear driving it in Manhattan. Finally, it occurs to me to check on the county of residence requirement, and I catch a break. It's about time. I can get a New York inspection anywhere in the state. I will not have to drive the van into Manhattan.

I make a plan. I will attach the New York plates in Austin and take a chance driving it from there to New York with a Texas inspection sticker. Even a first-class worrier like me can't get worked up about the possibility of a misdemeanor ticket. Then stop at the first inspection station we come to upon entering rural New York.

When we leave for Austin, I have on my mind nothing more challenging than getting the van started after we arrive there. Walle was not able to do that the last time he tried, though the battery was still strong. I will just call AAA if I have to. If the guy can't jump it, he and I will push it while Ann drives.

It's going to be a good trip down and a better trip back, even for one with a gift for worrying.

CHAPTER THIRTY
RECONCILIATION

While in Texas, we spend a weekend at the Osborns' ranch. One afternoon, Joe asks Ann and me to help him hang a livestock gate he had knocked off while driving the mule, a four-wheel-drive, all-terrain vehicle. We sign on eagerly. It's a way to play cowboy, keep the cattle in their proper pastures, and otherwise participate in ranch life. It turns out to be all that and more. It's a reminder of the elemental place cattle and ranching has in our lives despite the veganism we have adopted as adults. It speaks in the purifying effect of hard work, straining muscles, and sweat under a big sky. It could not be more different from our life in New York. The ambivalence we feel about Texas gives way to an unqualified sense of being one with the pasture and much of what it represents.

The steel gate is heavy, but the three of us can lift it. Nevertheless, it's exhausting to maneuver it so that the holes in the hinge (two near the top, two near the bottom) line up with the steel pins on the fence post. It requires holding the gate off the ground, one of us on the far end, which was fifteen or twenty feet from the hinge, one in the middle, and one on the end by the hinges. It has to be moved horizontally and vertically while at the same time getting the holes and pegs lined up at the same angle. The level of coordination required is almost more than we can manage, try as we do. We change positions from time to time, take breaks, and consider tactics. In my mind, I give up the effort long before it's over. So does Ann (notably when I lose my grip on the gate and it falls on her outstretched legs). Not Joe.

We are an unlikely crew of ranch hands – two skinny old men and a small gray-haired woman. Ann is sixty-five, I am eighty-two, Joe is eighty-nine. Joe, however, has an advantage; When he put on his old straw hat and worn boots, he became strong and youthful. He shed years as he bounced the mule up the rocky track to the gate. The short strides and tentative steps that are his and mine and most old men's are replaced by let's-get-it-done strides. The same metamorphosis happens during deer season when he puts on insulated camos, picks up a rifle, and heads out into the ranch in pursuit of game. He will keep us out there fixing the gate for days, if that's what it takes. He has driven up that hill to fix the thing, and no amount of difficulty is going to stop him.

He is being who he is – a man of the land. He grew up on a Texas Panhandle farm, milking cows, tending livestock, and doing chores, and it stayed with him. He is a voracious reader who spent fifty years as a lawyer, but he never stopped being the person who will sweat over gate repair on a hot afternoon in scrubby ranch land for however long it takes.

We finally get the gate back on its hinges, but that's not the end of the job; the latch has to be repaired. Fortunately, that's not difficult. Joe makes a temporary fix with a piece of electrical wire that happens to be in the mule. Later, Ann and I will be slugging down water and waiting for ibuprofen to take effect while he goes back up and does a better job using baling wire.

On the way from the gate back to the ranch house, he invites Ann to fuller participation in ranch life by driving the mule. It's a carnival-ride pleasure for her. And for him, too. There is a kind of intimacy in the moment.

The next afternoon, we pile in the mule for a tour of the ranch. There is a small grove of walnut trees where Joe had gotten lumber to make his desk, the remains of a nineteenth-century cabin and its well house, and some named springs. Cows and calves watch us from the shade of oak trees. There is a ready-for-prime-time longhorn and a lusty bull of great size and undoubtable prowess. Ann drives, smiling and confident, a Howard Hawks heroine.

Walle joins us for the tour despite his painful hip and sciatica. He grew up working summers on his older brothers' ranch. To a lesser extent, he's close to the land in the same way Joe is. And like Joe, his clock turns back as we bounce around in the mule. He becomes animated and smiling in a way that pain has made scarce in recent months.

As we're about to leave for Austin, we are held up by a dramatic thunderstorm with gale-force wind, lightning, and dark sky. Hard rain pounds on the tin roof of the front porch where we sit and watch it. Texas is not the only place where thunderstorms happen, but Texas would not be *our* Texas without a big one every so often.

It lets up after a couple of hours, and Ann and I drive out to the highway on the rough caliche road from the house.. On the way, we pass by a storm cellar owned by a practical neighbor. As we are nearing Austin, the storm reappears. This time it's more threatening. It has winds of seventy miles an hour, and hail the size of ping-pong balls is forecast.

I drive the van as far as possible into the Osborns' garage – it already has a car in it – and try to cover some of the exposed part with the empty Yakima luggage carrier. In the wind, it's impossible. I wrestle it into a shed behind the garage so that it doesn't get blown away, then fight my way up the outside stairs to the apartment over the garage where we are staying. The driving rain is blinding, and I'm so tired, I manage to reach the top only by pulling on the banister with my hands.

Rain, some of it heavy, continues off and on for the remaining ten days we're in Texas. It brings dry creeks and rivers to life causing low-water-crossing warnings. We pay attention to them as we get ready to visit our friend John, whose house is on the other side of a low-water crossing of the Pedernales River west of Austin. The flow past his house varies. Sometimes the riverbed is almost dry, but usually it has some water in it. Occasionally, it becomes deep and swift, covering the crossing to a height that makes it risky or impossible to drive through.

John stays in close touch as the time approaches for us to go out. The day before we are to try it, he emails that the river looks passable. It's unclear how long that will last, though. Showers are forecast all over the area upstream. He is going to a nearby town for groceries, and he'll let us know if he can't get back across to his house. If he can, he will have enough groceries to feed of us for some while, should Ann and I get in but can't get out. We do get in, and the river doesn't come up while we're there.

We spend a long afternoon and evening on the porch talking. The house faces east, and we watch the river as the sun sets behind us. John points to a rock that he uses as a depth marker. He can see a line on it – Ann and I can't – which is the high-water mark. I suggest he add a decibel meter to his measurement tools. In dry weather, the sound of the river goes mostly unnoticed. Today, it will not be denied. Not too loud, though. Not threatening. Just a reminder of its presence.

We talk politics, climate change, natural resources, water tables, well depths, the environmental damage of a nearby pipeline project. We tell old stories. A deer or two put in appearances. Hummingbirds swarm around a row of feeders. When it gets dark, foxes come trick or treating, one at a time, to beg dog biscuits.

In the morning, we take a walk along the river to see what changes the high water has brought. Sometimes furniture and other items float downstream and come to rest on John's shore. This time we find only a fire extinguisher. We study animal tracks in the mud. John hopes to see some made by raccoons, but there are none. Their tracks have become scarce, and he and a neighbor are concerned.

The Austin visit has been much to our liking, including as it did, celebration of old friendships and happy visits with family. Just about everything comes down on the positive side of our love/hate attitude toward Texas. Prevailing political views and culture are as odious as ever, but the land is still the land, and the objectionable stuff is put into perspective by hot work in a pasture, flooded low-water crossings, and conversations full of unqualified trust and respect over long meals with loving friends.

Developments with the van have been similarly restorative. When I arrived at the storage facility, I got it started without aid of AAA. The battery was still strong, and I just kept cranking the engine till it came to life. It was a small victory, but small counts, especially to a worrier. Another one followed. I had been afraid that the screws on the Texas license plates would be rusted and require more than a screwdriver to remove. They came loose easily. I put on the New York plates, drove around to the office, and closed the account. I had expected driving the van would be hard after so long not doing it, but I quickly got comfortable again.

One afternoon when the rain lets up, Ann and I drive to a shady park and apply the German wax we'd bought in California. It's a tiring, two-hour job, but when we finish, the van is gleaming, and it attracts more than the usual number of appreciative waves and smiles and conversations. In a shopping center, a man pulls up beside us in a 1939 Chevrolet and asks if the van has a Porsche engine. (I guess the question was prompted by its uncharacteristic rumble.) It introduces one of those hearty chats between members of the society of old-car enthusiasts. In the course of it, he says, "You could get $100,000 for that thing." Exaggerated as the figure is, I like hearing it. On some days, I might have joked that I accept checks, but not this one.

For the first time in a long while – maybe ever – owning the van feels not so much like a chore as a pleasure. The feeling grows after I get a locking cable for the Yakima luggage carrier so that I won't have to unload and reload it at motels. Other worry antidotes follow. I send gear we won't need to Vic and Pam, making more space in the van. My son Teo tells me about a rechargeable battery that will power lights and laptops and phones for as long as several days. Just the thing to have where no hookups are available as in Great Smoky Mountains National Park where we are going to spend a few days. Tom has a solution for keeping the battery charged through a New Hampshire winter – a battery tender. It costs less than forty dollars and requires only to be connected to a power source, like plugging in a lamp.

We drive out of Austin happy, optimistic, unafraid of the van's age-related frailties, and renewed, even reconciled. I am a new me – in regard to the van and much else. But not entirely. Do Vic and Pam turn off their electricity when they leave New Hampshire in winter? I don't ask. I'll find out when we get there. If they do, I'll figure out something. I've been able to do that with everything that has come up so far.

CHAPTER THIRTY-ONE
A DAY IN THE DELTA

A middle-aged man in a crisp parks-department uniform is wearing rubber gloves and carrying a bucket and toilet brush. He is cleaning the restrooms at Martin Creek Lake State Park in northeast Texas.

"Good morning. It can't be much fun cleaning other people's toilets."

He smiles. "If I don't do it, it ain't gonna get done."

"Well, thank you."

The restroom would pass the most careful inspection. The whole park is clean and well-maintained. We spend an enjoyable evening and night there and have a short walk around the lake next morning.

The van is loaded with everything we need for the twelve weeks until the apartment renovation is complete. So, to sleep in it requires a good deal of unloading.

The campsite has a picnic table under a roof, and we pile most of our gear there, taking care not to leave food out when we turn in. But in the middle of the night, we are wakened by banging of pans and dishes. I knew that raccoons are clever scavengers with big appetites, but I'm surprised to learn that they like coffee. We bring it into the van, go back to sleep, brew some in the morning, take hot showers in the tidy restrooms, and push on, refreshed and looking forward to the next stop – Leroy Percy State Park, seventy miles north of Vicksburg, Mississippi.

The drive across Louisiana on Interstate 20 has little to recommend it, but we expect more interesting driving after crossing the Mississippi River and turning onto two-lane Rt. 61. Before doing that, we mean to stop for some supper things, and other odds and ends, including gas, at a store outside Vicksburg, but we miss it. It's to the south, and I, the navigator on duty, direct Ann to drive north.

The area between Vicksburg and the park is sparsely settled farmland, mostly cotton, I think, with cultivated fields stretching to the Mississippi levee. There are few towns and gas stations, and the faulty gas gauge drops to near what might or might not be empty. We consider going back to Vicksburg, but believing that the dots on the map that indicate small towns will have a station, we keep going.

We're getting close to major inconvenience and another call to AAA – one that will probably cause them to rate us the way insurance companies sometimes do after too many claims – when we come upon an isolated, one-room post office at a crossroad. *Yes.* Post offices and fire stations can always provide directions. I ask the only clerk where the nearest station is. She shrugs and says, "I'm not from around here." So much for my belief about post offices.

An idling delivery truck is parked nearby. The driver looks up from some paperwork when I knock on his window.

"What direction you headed?"

"North."

He looks off into the distance for a moment. "How low are you?"

"Real."

He shakes his head. "Well, you better go back south. The nearest one is a little grocery store about twelves miles back."

Twelve miles? There is a good chance we can't make it that far.

He senses my anxiety. "Don't worry. I'll be going that way myself in about ten minutes. I'll be right behind you. If you run out, I'll take care of you."

I wonder if he knows Cindy, the water-bearing angel.

We turn around and drive back the way we just came, keeping our speed at about thirty to conserve fuel, feeling relieved, but also a little contrite about our fearfulness. The good feelings start to fade as we pass "about twelve miles" without seeing anything but the road. Then at seventeen miles, a small frame store with peeling paint and dusty pumps appears. The ghostly gas station along the Columbia River comes to mind. How much repetition is the day going to hold? Not so much, it turns out. This time, the pumps don't work. I try to go into the store to ask about them, but the door is locked. I rattle the screen and peer into windows. Eventually, a young woman appears.

"Sorry. I was out back."

I ask about the pumps.

"Oh, we don't sell gas anymore" She pauses like an actor seeking dramatic effect. "But you can get some over there." She points across the road and a little farther on to a run-down store much like her own. It doesn't look like a gas station. I guess she can see my skepticism. She points again, and changes to a little more insistent tone. "Right there."

It has a worn pump that dispenses regular-grade gas. No middle-grade. No high octane. The van does better on high octane, but it's not a time to be picky. It takes 11.1 gallons. I've never been sure what its capacity is, but I think it holds thirteen. We must not have been as close to running out as we'd feared.

When we get to an internet signal, I look online for an exact figure, but I can't find it. I contact Tom later, and he says 15.9. Clearly, it's time to fix that gauge. But maybe not. Working properly, it would have deprived us of the truck driver's kindly offhand rebuke of faithless fear and worldly anxiety. I watch closely for him to drive by, so I can wave my thanks. He never appears. We probably weren't watching closely enough. Or maybe he had not driven south at all, just told us that so we would be encouraged.

No one is tending the entrance to Leroy Percy Park, but we know the number of our campsite, so we drive right to it. The general look of the grounds is not very park-like, just open space dotted with grills, water hydrants, and power outlets mounted on poles. There are no tents in sight, just a few RVs. Our site is next to one There is no roof over the picnic table. All in all, it's about as inviting as a homeless encampment, but I hook up the power connection and unload a few things while Ann goes to check the restrooms, which are some distance away. She brings back a negative review of the facilities, just as it starts to rain.

We saddle up and go look for supper and a motel, settling finally on a Hampton Inn an hour or so away in Yazoo City. We arrive there hungry and tired and in no mood to drive around looking for it. Name-brand motels usually have billboards with directions on the highway into towns. If the Hampton Inn has one, we miss it. I stop in a beer-and-lottery-tickets convenience store and ask directions. A young customer answers eagerly. Yazoo City is a small town. Population just under twelve thousand. But you wouldn't know that from the complicated directions the guy gives me. And I'm so tired, that by the time I'm getting back in the van, all I can remember is that I should go southeast and circle halfway around the courthouse.

The helpful customer is right behind me. "I'll show you," he says. "Just follow me."

He and another man get in an old car that badly needs a muffler. I hope we make it to the motel without witnessing one of those traffic stops of the sort we see on television. The young men are black, and they have an air freshener and something else hanging from their rear-view mirror. We wind our way through downtown and around the courthouse and past grand old houses and after a quarter of an hour pull up in front of the motel without incident.

The rest of the evening does not go so well. As in most motels, the air conditioning in our room has made it cold enough to freeze the plumbing. The thermostat doesn't work, and the look of the place suggests it's unlikely there will be an evening maintenance person. We put on the few warm clothes we've brought with us, have a drink, nuke microwave dinners, and turn on the tv to divert ourselves with something – almost anything – until bedtime. No matter what we do, though, the screen remains blank. I call the front desk several times but get no answer. It doesn't seem even to be ringing. I go down and take a place in the line of people who are checking in. When my turn comes, the young clerk starts taking phone calls.

I say, "I thought your phone was out of order."

"No. It works fine. I'm just the only one here."

I tell her the tv won't come on. She writes down my room number and says she will come have a look when she gets a chance. I go back upstairs, have another drink, and go to bed.

I start the next day thinking about the truck driver on Rt 61 and the guys who'd been our harbor pilots through the city. Their actions count as much as the shortcomings of Leroy Percy Park or poor management of a small-town motel.

CHAPTER THIRTY-TWO
CAMPING

Next up is Tims Ford State Park in south central Tennessee. (There is no apostrophe because "Tims" is the surname of a man for whom the park is named.) In the morning while drinking coffee, I come across some comments about the park, including, "badly in need of upgrading." I tell Ann what I've read, and we agree to skip it and find something more to our liking. For the first time in a long while, Ann has taken a week off from work. We are in vacation mode, and it includes camping. But not at Leroy Percy or Tims Ford.

A few hours on the Natchez Trace Parkway are a splendid realization of the concept of "vacation." The Parkway is a winding, two-lane road that runs 440 miles from Natchez to Nashville. It has been there a long time. Prehistoric indigenous peoples used it and built settlements along its path. Native Americans traveled it for centuries. In the eighteenth century, Europeans began to use it for commerce. In the early nineteenth century, commerce grew as it became possible to use wagons on the Trace, and it became a link between ports on the Mississippi and the developed eastern part of the country. Inns called stands were built along the Trace, and what's left of them is well marked. To drive slowly (fast is not possible) on the Trace taking in some of many historical markers is to be nudged back in time and away from busy, technology-dominant current day.

The van seems made for such driving; the Trace seems made for the van. The variation of forest and open pastures taken in through the open windows of a mystique-bearing, plodding relic is liberating in the way we had imagined when we first had the urge to buy a VW van. We have had too little of that to this point. Dealing with obstacles and seemingly being unable not to hurry and driving too many miles each day had been our lot much of the time. Before the Natchez Trace, we'd had one such sort of transcendent moment when driving alongside the Oregon Trail and plenty of good times, but not enough of this unwound calm.

For the first time, we realize that owning this camper does not require camping. It's possible to sleep in it, but we don't have to. Who knew? Nor or we required to use the tent. If we never set it up, so what? Much of the pleasure of traveling about in a classic VW camper exists apart from that. We've been bullied about by trying too hard to live the life depicted in VW ads from the seventies. Mom is wearing a twin set, Dad smokes a pipe and looks manly, kids are sleeping in the hammock over the main bunk. They smile idiotically. Besides that, we were always only making believe we were pot-smoking free spirits. Still, our VW style is way cool.

Going forward, the nature of our VW van experience will be less burdened by self-inflicted demands.

We get off the Trace after a time, cross a corner of Alabama, then stop for the night in Pulaski, Tennessee, at a fully functional motel and enjoy a comfortable king-size bed. Being there has none of the vague sense of failure that motel stays in the past have evoked. Anyway, it's a last hurrah before three days of camping in Great Smoky Mountains National Park, which doesn't have hot water or showers.

We arrive at the park after the ranger who handles check-ins has gone off duty, and we don't know which site we have. After some exploration, we find the Camp Hosts, a couple who live in a mobile home and take care of things like late arrivals.

"It's right across the road," Mr. Camp Host says.

All I see is a wide spot in the road. I walk over for a closer look, and there it is. Down a steep incline from the road is a picnic table, grill, firepit, and a hard surface on which to pitch a tent. All as advertised, provided you have a burro or a sherpa to hump your gear up and down the slope. It's so steep, I fall twice, once while carrying a first-cup-of-the-morning hot coffee. Not good. Also, the online description indicated that the site has water, but I don't see any. Oh well, the bathroom is a short walk away. I can get water there. Not so fast. The water in the bathroom is not potable. Potable water is down the road. Not far, but too far to walk carrying much water. There, a single spigot serves multiple campsites in a kind of village-well arrangement.

For the first time I can recall, I rate something the federal government does as inferior to that of a Texas effort. Martin Creek Lake State Park is clearly preferable.

I stumble down the slope with camp chairs, propane stove, and other gear so that we will have room to open the van's bed. We turn in early and don't raise the pop-up roof. It rains during the night, but I make no attempt to lug the stuff back up the slope. It will survive. Anyway, with the bed open, there is hardly room inside the van for it.

The rain has stopped by morning, so I fire up the stove, make coffee, and have two cups – all while standing up. Chairs and table are too wet to sit in. But the sun comes out boldly after a bit, and we set about exploring the park. A long walk along Deep Creek takes us past three dramatic waterfalls. We had thought we would hike to a place called Sassafras Gap. We had read a little (too little) about it, and the name had a come-hither ring. We don't have a map, so I ask a man who is wearing what appears to be a new outfit made up of everything Orvis sells for the well-dressed fly fisherman. He is quite the dude. Even his five-day growth of beard seems to be part of the Orvis look.

"How far is it to Sassafras Gap?" He doesn't answer for a while; his mouth is holding line he's tying a fly with. When he finishes, he says, "About twenty-four miles."

We turn back, and along the way enjoy watching people having a classic good time riding the creek's current on tubes under towering trees on a warm day. By the time we get back to our campsite, we have walked for a couple of hours, and the trail was hilly, so we're tired. After lunch, we nod off – I, sitting up in a now-dry camp chair, Ann, sitting up in the van, the bed having been folded away for the day. We had planned to put up the tent after our rest, but when we come to, it's spitting rain again and promising more. We put up the top of the van instead. It creates more room for storing gear, and it makes it a little easier to scrunch in and out of the sleeping berth. As we finish setting it to rights, thunder and lightning begin, followed by hard, wind-driven rain. It storms all night.

For the first time in months, my prostate is acting up. In the storm, the restroom might as well be in the next county. I step a decent distance from the van (about three steps actually) take up a position there and try to pass urine, wishing the wind would stop changing directions, and trying not to howl into the storm like King Lear. When I do go over to the bathroom in the morning, I am so wet and sleep deprived, it occurs to me that I might have been better off sleeping there, curled up on the floor like a homeless person.

At around daylight, the storm lets up. We don't wait around for it to start again. It has been a singularly unpleasant night, and we'd sweated so much the day before we need a shower, and a rear wheel on the van has begun making a threatening sound. We load up and drive on.

We had planned to take the north-south road from one perimeter of the park to the other and enjoy the mountain scenery. But the fog is so thick we wouldn't see anything, and the van might not be up to it; a problem with the rear wheel is growing more threatening. In the first town outside the park, we find a place that has opened early, get coffee and a roll, and drive on slowly, looking for an internet signal so we can search for the nearest old-VW shop.

It turns out to be in Asheville, but it's not open yet. We can wait for it to open, but there is no reason to assume they will be able to help us immediately. It can take days to get an appointment at an old-VW shop. There is another shop in Durham, where we are planning to spend a week visiting my son Ben and his family. It's three hundred miles away, but whatever the risk, it's preferable to waiting and doing nothing but imagining the worst.

First, though, we have to get out of the mountains. It's a low-gear effort on twisting roads with engine-straining ascents and scary downhill runs – just the sort of thing to avoid in a failing antique van. The challenge grows when fog thickens and enshrouds us like a whiteout. It turns the calendar back fifty-three years, and I'm facing the possibility of death in the Chevrolet station wagon in a blizzard on the mountain pass between Damascus and Beirut. I have an urge to tell Ann the story, but I don't. She's heard it too many times already.

We wait for the fog to lift. There is no shoulder, and we just stop where we are – maybe in the right lane, maybe in the left, maybe in the middle of the road – there is no way to know for sure. We turn on the flashers and persuade ourselves that we are not likely to be smashed by oncoming traffic because like us it has probably stopped to let the fog clear.

We emerge from the mountains unharmed, but we still have to get through several hours of freeway driving. The noise from the wheel is increasing, and on the highway, decelerating feels like engine braking.

CHAPTER THIRTY-THREE
"DAD" COMES TO DURHAM

For a while after getting to Durham, we think about little else than how lucky we are to have made it without having to wait on the side of a highway for a tow truck and a big repair bill. After that flushes out of our systems, many signs point to a mean week.

On the first morning, I join Ann for a short walk. It's on relatively flat ground and the temperature is mild. We move along at a moderate pace, but I have dead legs. Either the Smoky Mountain interlude has been enervating or I'm sick. Either way, rest is called for.

The house we've rented through SabbaticalHomes.com lacks soap (both hand and dishwashing). The furniture is worn. It doesn't have a coffee maker. Television watching is limited to Hulu and other services we don't want to have to puzzle our way into.

For the first time in two and a half years, my back acts up. It's to be expected, I suppose, after twisting in and out of the van's bunk and neglecting my exercises, but I can't help worrying that it might be a recurrence of the problem that had required surgery two and a half years earlier. The pain is not so severe that Tramadol, rest, and sitting up straight can't keep it under control – but it's enough to give me a bad attitude.

An odd tech problem is among the swarm of locusts that is forming. Neither of us can get our phones or laptops to charge.

And always playing in the background is anxiety about the van.

* * * *

I arrive at the VW shop at a little before five on Friday, hoping to persuade them to give me some indication of whether we are likely to breakdown if I keep driving the van until they have time to fix it. I fear an exchange such as "Yup. That sounds like bad bearings. Better leave it with us till we can get to you in a couple of weeks." Or better, but unlikely, "Just needs some grease. Let me give it a squirt." Either answer would require them not to go hostile when they spot the New York license plates. New York does not play well in the south, perhaps not even in progressive Durham.

When I describe the problem to the man on the desk, he seems never to have heard of such symptoms. And he doesn't seem interested. Doesn't talk much either. Then he surprises me. He emerges from the little nest of gun-rights signs and anti-tax slogans that is his office, drives the van into an open bay, and pries off a hub cap. Rattling around in it are the broken bits of the cotter pin, the last line of defense when the inner workings of the wheel are so messed up that the wheel is about to fall off. "You were lucky," he says, shaking his head. He takes the wheel off and pokes around for a few minutes. By five o'clock closing, he has applied a temporary fix.

"Can I drive it this way?"

"You *can*, but..."

I take a chance and drive it around town without incident until Monday, when the shop happens to have an opening.

Before leaving on Friday, I'm treated to the origin story. The owner started working on VWs in the sixties. His son, the man on the desk, has been at it for about twenty-five years. The owner points at an old man who is sitting at a table working on an engine in front of him., "He still had hair when he started." I think he says the man's name is Duke. Duke grins. I want to ask how many times they have performed this routine, but I think better of it.

When the show is over, I try to pay.

"Naw, we'll take care of it Monday," Junior says.

"You don't even know my name."

"That don't matter," Junior says.

When I arrive at 8:01 on Monday morning, Duke is in the same place doing the same thing as when I left on Friday. I suppose he had not been there all weekend, but it sure seems that way.

He glances up at me over his glasses, says something I don't understand, and keeps working.

"When the whistle blows, you get right to work, don't you." He smiles and keeps picking at the engine. I find a broken-down office chair, sit in it, and wait for something to happen.

After ten minutes or so, I venture, "You the only one here?'

"Yup."

I keep sitting.

After another ten minutes or so, I retreat to the van to listen to *Morning Edition*, preferring even the insufferable Steve Inskeep to the country music playing inside. I'm beginning to question this view, when Duke comes out a little while later.

It's good he can work sitting down sometimes. He is hunched, and he takes the short, slow steps – sort of a shuffle – of an old man. He pulls the van inside and goes to work on it. I resume my place in the broken-down office chair and watch. He takes off the problem wheel, then some other components, then the other wheel. I get up once and go over for a close look, but the sight of all those parts spread out on the floor is a little alarming. At his age, Duke might not be able to remember how to put them back together.

I go back to my chair. Duke shuffles around the shop now and then looking for tools and parts, but mostly he stays under the van, steady as sin. While he works, I nod off, secure in the sense of being taken care of, albeit in a peculiar way.

Around 9:30 a man and a woman come in.

"Anybody here?" the man asks.

I point at Duke. "Just him."

They take up a position behind me and stand there a good half an hour not saying anything. Then the man shouts at Duke, "OK if I go in the parts department and look around?"

Duke says, "Sure."

Pretty soon, he comes out carrying something in a shrink-wrapped package and leaves. I guess he and Duke know each other.

After a while, Junior shows up. I hear him tell a customer that he's late because he had driven his dad to get his cataracts "taken off." It sounds like something you'd do to a car.

Around 11:30, Duke puts the wheels back on and shuffles over to his worktable. He says, "you goin' on back up to Yankee land now?" I feel like a member of an exotic species. The feeling grows when, as Junior is adding up the charges, he asks me why I live "up there."

I just say, "New York's not for everybody, but I like it." He doesn't look strong enough to handle the full treatment.

I pay and leave, grateful and relieved that the van is fixed and hoping that my presence has given Duke and Junior something to make their world a little bigger and more interesting. They surely have done that for me.

It's an indication that the warning signs at the beginning of the week were wrong.

The house we've rented continues to have shortcomings, but being there becomes interesting and enjoyable in an unexpected way. It seems to be situated on a large lot, but it's difficult to know for sure. The back and side yards run on into surrounding yards without interruption by a fence or any obvious property lines. A large expanse – a couple of acres, maybe more – stretches out toward the house to the rear. In the middle of the yard are some kind of fruit trees. Along one side is waist-high grass like fens, a private place for rabbits and deer when they aren't browsing in the open. One morning, we are treated to a show by a new-born fawn. It kicks up its heels like a bucking horse, hops up and down like a gamboling lamb, then races about fifty yards in one direction, turns around and races back to the starting point, repeats, nuzzles against its mother, rests a moment, then starts its joyous dance again.

The deer share the space with two teenage girls who alternately sunbathe and work in a vegetable garden. They also tend the two hens our landlord keeps in a backyard coop. With the landlord's approval, we take part in the chickens' care, letting them out to roam and herding them back inside in the evening, if the girls have not. I give the hens some stale bread, and afterward they all but come to the door and ask if I can come out and play. When I sit on the back porch trying to write, they join me, clucking and begging for more. I retreat to the front porch, and they find me there. When clucking and staring at me doesn't get them what they want, they peck my feet and pants cuffs. I feed them a lot while we are there. It seems like the right thing to do; we eat their eggs.

The neighborhood looks like a hastily constructed subdivision but not exactly. The houses are fairly similar and have been built around the same time, perhaps in the sixties. They are big houses on big lots, but they are unpretentious. Unfenced yards are common as in the house where we are staying. Many have vegetable gardens.

It's a quiet neighborhood with little racket from power mowers and leaf blowers, which are the scourge of most well-kept, upscale neighborhoods. One evening, I see a half dozen or so cars park in front of the house next to ours. I fear the disturbance that must surely be coming. Guests gather on the patio, which is quite close to where I'm sitting reading. All I hear is quiet conversation and occasional laughter – amiable, civil, grown-up. Can a good party exist absent amplified music and loud talk? That one does.

Neighbors drop by our place from time to time for one reason or another. We encounter a teenage boy in the garage, getting out the lawnmower. While Ann and I are waxing the van one day, a man stops in to talk vintage cars. Another neighbor trims shrubbery along the driveway while we come and go. It's as if we are sharing the house with whoever wants. For the most part, that feels good, but one night after Ann and I are in bed reading and almost asleep, the doorbell rings. We try to ignore it, but it continues. When we hear the garage door opening, Ann dresses and goes down. A man is inside.

"Hello," he says. "I came to return a tool."

One night when I was sleeping, my father, dead for fifty-seven years, comes by. I suppose he may have been drawn to the prevailing peacefulness of the place. At his death, he and I had unresolved issues. I did, at least. He may not have. I have spent the years since thinking of things I wish I had said and ways I wish I had been. When he drops by in Durham, I say, "Hello, Dad." During his life on earth, he had always been "Daddy," never "Dad." He is surprised to see me.

"Paul," he says. We embrace. Decades of regret and recrimination fall away.

CHAPTER THIRTY-FOUR
TWO-LANE BLACKTOP

The most direct route between Durham and Woodstock, New York, our next stop, is a long one-day drive on Interstates, and on the north end, it includes jousting with the traffic around Newark Airport and time in the purgatory of the New Jersey Turnpike. It's not for us. The few hours on the Natchez Trace left its mark. We drive farther, take two days, and mostly stay off of Interstates. In the beginning, it's much like driving the Natchez Trace – leisurely and scenic, the Blue Ridge Mountains to the east and rolling pastures and horse farms to the west. Around noon, I spoil the fun.

Now that Covid restrictions have become less limiting, America has taken to the road. It's as if everyone is desperate to get out and drive somewhere. That year of being penned up was awful, and who knows when it might start again. As a consequence, motel rooms are not readily available. Waiting till late in the day to decide where to stop and sleep is apt to result in a night in Cockroach Courts, or if it's Saturday, maybe in the car. So, while Ann is driving in the morning, I get right on it. "No vacancy" appears over and over on my laptop screen.

I cast my net wider, and that works. I find a nice upmarket accommodation. It's a little pricey, but that is to be expected in these times. I feel good about my success. I read a description of it to Ann, and she feels good about it. My sense of triumph lasts about five minutes, which is how long it takes me to realize that I've made a reservation in a city that is two or three hundred miles out of the way. And – this is important – I have declined to pay the moderate fee to make the reservation cancellable.

I keep this to myself for as long as I can. I persuade Ann to stop at the first gas station we come to because I really need to pee, which I don't. I just want to phone the motel without being overheard as I beg the nice lady who answers to cancel my uncancellable reservation. She can't do that. Only Travelocity can. Maybe Travelocity will and maybe it won't. I'll never know. Travelocity does not want to talk to customers on the phone, so they hide their number. I never do find one.

I confess to Ann. There is no way to spin my transgression artfully enough to make it acceptable, but I try. I fall back on my training in linguistics and explain that the error is a common type widely studied and described in academic journals. It happens when two words have the same focal vowel. They are easily confused. Scholars know it as "vocalic override syndrome." I had fallen victim to it. Ann rolls her eyes and sighs.

I try, "Anyone could have made this mistake when tired and also distracted by gorgeous scenery." No response.

And "Using an iPhone in a moving vehicle on a winding road is going to increase the likelihood of errors."

"The wrong city?"

The event would have been resulted in even more contention, but for my keeping to myself the name of the city where we were going to pay for a fairly expensive motel room but not stay in it. In fact, at the time, I gave a somewhat understated indication of how big my mistake was in terms of mileage. And I'm not revealing the name of the city here.

Ann is understandably unhappy about what I have done, and I'm ashamed and embarrassed. But by midafternoon, both of us are putting it behind us. The beauty of our surroundings and driving through small towns of Virginia reading historic markers has a restorative effect.

The next day, we delight in a slow drive through northeast Pennsylvania, the Southern Tier of New York, the Catskills, and on into Woodstock. We had been in the Catskills once many years earlier on an afternoon visit to look at a house we were considering buying. We saw the house and the highway we drove on to get to it and little else. We could have been in any low mountains anywhere in the country. Apart from that experience, the Catskills mean to us the Borscht Belt of the early twentieth century with its many hotels where northeastern Jews spent months in the summer laughing at Sid Caesar, Henny Youngman, and other comedians.

A slow few hours following along the upper reaches of the Delaware offer a different picture. When George Washington took his troops across the Delaware some miles downstream, the river was freezing, dark, menacing, and wide. The Delaware of our afternoon is an idyllic, sun-speckled trout stream, rippling quietly alongside a bower-like, tree-covered lane that is unspoiled by crowds of tourists.

Woodstock, too, belies expectations, but in a less welcome way. It's not nearly as charming as we thought it would be.

In the first place, the hippie fest by that name took place forty miles away near the town of Ulster.

Thinking that the sight of the van would call forth a stir of nostalgic recognition was misguided. I imagined we would take a place of honor in a July 4 parade. There is no 4th of July parade.

Nor is it the quiet rural redoubt we had imagined. Its little downtown is crowded with pedestrians and choked with automobile traffic. It's more Times Square than Grover's Corners. The main street, essentially the only street, is lined with shops seeking to separate tourists from their money by selling "art," tie-dyed garments, crystals, Tarot readings, tattoos, and many kinds of kitsch. Overpriced, understaffed restaurants and cafes specialize in food of mediocre quality. The village is as inauthentic as if it had built from a kit.

It does have, however, a CVS, a health food store, and a bakery that makes excellent bread. They are the only reasons we can find to go into the downtown. Not even the weekly farmer's market is sufficient enticement; it's short on parking spaces.

We are in Woodstock for six weeks. That's a long time to be in a place you don't much like. But thanks be, other aspects of our life there are at least a mixed bag.

The village is surrounded by densely green, low mountains, and a clear stream runs past the house, murmuring and gurgling insistently when rain brings its level up and turns the water brown. But these pluses require qualification. Gnats and some kind of flying insects are a nuisance. Unlike blackflies, the season for which is over, they don't bite, but taking a walk involves a lot of arm waving, like a cow swishing its tail, to keep them out of your eyes, mouth, and ears. We enjoy daily walks despite the bugs. It rains frequently, and the creatures don't come out during showers. We do. Walking in rain has always been to our liking – more so when it drives away bugs.

The three-bedroom house we've rented is historic, badly in need of repair, quirky, and in some ways charming. In other ways, it was a regrettable choice.

The most enjoyable room is a screened porch, which seems to have been added to the house after it was built. It's at the back of the house and looks onto a sprawling lawn ringed by tall trees. Most mornings, I take a seat on it and enjoy the first light of day. Meditation and mindfulness and such are much in vogue these days. Inexplicably, people pay to be taught how to do it. For me, it's simply what happens when, for a while, you don't talk, and you eliminate distractions. A half hour or so of that on a screened porch in a forest in early morning sun is uplifting, refreshing, and quieting.

When morning is fully underway, woodchucks appear on the lawn. One little guy has a den in a stump close to where I sit. He usually sleeps late. The other day, he emerged at around ten, stretched and yawned in a woodchucky kind of way, then scurried over to the trees, where I suppose his bathroom is. He came back after a bit, had a hearty brunch of grass made especially green and delicious by the rain we've been having, then hopped up on the top of his stump and slipped away into a morning snooze in the warm sun, pleased, I'm sure, that it was not raining for a change.

Woodchucks share the property with half-tame deer. Most are does. A couple of them have fawns. In early evening, a buck pays a visit to the front of the house. He emerges out of a thicket and swaggers across the lawn. One time at a Yankees game, I saw Derek Jeter and Alex Rodriquez move just like that on the way from the dugout to their positions in the infield. My buck has ten points (still in velvet), so naturally he is full of himself. He goes to the apple tree by the front door as if it had been planted there for his particular enjoyment. At this time of year, the apples show only a little color. They must be pretty sour. My buck likes them, though. After he's done there, he comes closer and tops off his dinner with ferns that grow next to where Ann and I are having cocktails, only a pain of glass between us and him. He looks directly at us, curious and fearless, then swaggers off into the trees.

One afternoon when Ann and I are on the screened porch reading, Ann says something to me dramatically *sotto voce*. "There's a bear over there," she says motioning with her head. It's about half-grown. It moves along at an easy pace stopping part way across the yard, as if to give us a chance to take some pictures, if we happen to have a camera in hand, which we don't – just passing through on his way to somewhere in the trees beyond.

The house is furnished with knick-knacks, family treasures, and furniture that have been accumulating for a long time. How long I can't say, but many years. And books, lots and lots of books. There is what seems to be a complete set of Dickens, three shelves and more of classic children's books, an odd lot of eighteenth and nineteenth century English fiction. All are arranged alphabetically, except for here and there some chick-lit titles adrift in the sea of classics.

I sample the collection randomly. Some titles get serious, even studious reading, especially *The Wind in the Willows*. I read it to my boys when they were young and later on my own, but in the past, I didn't notice the few pages in which Water Rat has a mystical experience. It's an experience beyond words, and the author, Kenneth Grahame, acknowledges that. Nevertheless, he has a go at it and does a pretty good job.

I try a couple of Trollop stories, but I can't connect with them. I rarely read short stories; I suppose Trollop is not a promising place to try to change my way. I am, however, engaged by two stories from a different time and place by Flannery O'Connor. Two are enough, though. One stormy evening, I take a plunge into an illustrated edition of *Ivanhoe*. The lengthy, colorful descriptions and character sketches are a delight, but they go on for so many pages, I despair of finishing it before senility sets in. When Ann points out that there is a 1952 film of *Ivanhoe* with Elizabeth Taylor and Robert Taylor, I put the book back in its place. We find the film on a streaming channel and watch it on my laptop. I turn to *Robinson Crusoe*, and I read it in full. I can't see why it's highly regarded, though. Maybe I'm just not sophisticated enough. I turn last to the 1946 Rieu translation of *The Odyssey*. I don't finish it before it's time to pack up and move on. I'll buy a copy when we get back to New York and read it alongside the more recent, highly regarded translation in verse by Robert Fagles, which has languished for several years in an ever-growing "one of these days" pile.

The house leaves a great deal to be desired as a house. Screens are torn. Wallpaper is stained from years of roof leaks. Most rooms are dark. And over it all as a sort of pall is the owner's sad illusion that it's the equal of Schönbrunn Palace. Nevertheless, to be allowed to rent it, we had to be interviewed (via Zoom) despite having already passed through the SabbaticalHomes.com selection process. When we arrived, we had to submit to what the owner referred to grandly as a "tour." She was guided through the exercise by several pages of longhand notes. It included everything from which lights must not be used to instruction to park the van several inches away from the grass but not so far away that driveway traffic is impeded. (Despite using a list and going on for about an hour, she omitted letting us know that the kitchen counters will be decorated with mouse poop each morning.)

She grew up in the house and still lives in it. When guests rent it, she retreats to an apartment in the barn about fifty feet away. Her presence, whether physical or just sensed, is oppressive. Despite all that, it's a deeply comfortable place to spend an evening in a club chair reading and listening to rain.

While we're in Woodstock, I drive the van to the next town, Kingston, and find a shop that does state inspections. I still do not completely believe that the rules allow for inspections outside the county you live in, so I'm a little apprehensive. The garage owner is grumpy, and he worries me from the start. I hand him the registration papers I wrested from the DMV in Harlem. He tears them apart, which I take as a bad sign. But then he gives one piece back to me and tells me to keep it in the glove box.

Part way through the inspection, he asks me if there is a switch to activate the back-up lights. I'm no help to him; I'm not aware it has back-up lights. Anyway, if they exist, shouldn't they come on when the van is in reverse? I go off to one side and search the internet, while he continues working.

I hear him say to one of his mechanics that the light over the license plate is out. Alarm bells sound. Buying a new one could be difficult. I could order one, but while waiting for it to arrive, I'd have to continue driving around with the Texas sticker, which, to compound my crime, is now way out-of-date. My thoughts touch on bribery. It had been on offer once years ago in the Bronx when an inspection didn't go well. I pace around outside the shop until a mechanic comes out and says. "I can't get it into reverse. Will you come in here and drive it out?" I do, and in the process, I see a beautiful New York sticker on the windshield. The garage happened to have the license plate bulb, and the missing back-up lights had not been mentioned again.

I drive back to Woodstock and the ramshackle old house full of books feeling a weight lifted. The sticker is the next to last problem the van will present. The final one, getting the battery tender to work correctly when I store it in New Hampshire with Vic and Pam is minor, even to my way of thinking.

Life without a seemingly unsolvable van problem is going to take some getting used to.

AFTERWORD

A few days more than two years after we shut the door of the Austin condo and set out to have some fun, we park the van in our friends' barn in New Hampshire where it will spend the winter months. We test the battery tender and find it working as intended.

We look forward to visiting Vic and Pam in fair weather, especially during autumn when leaves turn. We'll clean the van outside and in, wax it, change the oil, put air in the tires, and drive slowly around New England for a few days. More sometimes. Maybe we'll camp some. Might even put up the tent. Maybe not. It doesn't matter. We'll chug along enjoying the way of van travel we had realized on the Natchez Trace.

Between outings, we will be at home in New York City.

Don't miss out!

Visit the website below and you can sign up to receive emails whenever PAUL WILLCOTT publishes a new book. There's no charge and no obligation.

https://books2read.com/r/B-A-UYZS-DLVZB

BOOKS 2 READ

Connecting independent readers to independent writers.

Also by PAUL WILLCOTT

Annals of Franklin Manor
A Franklin Manor Christmas
A Franklin Manor Epiphany

Standalone
12,000 Miles of Road Thoughts. Old Van, Old Man, Recovering
Hippie, Dying Cat
In Passing. Scenes from an Unconventional Life

Watch for more at paulwillcott.com.

About the Author

Paul Willcott is a lapsed Texan with four degrees from the University of Texas, including a Ph.D. in applied linguistics and a law degree. He is a retired newspaper columnist, award-winning blogger, novelist, and one-poem poet.

He has lived in Baghdad, Amman, Tehran, London, Hong Kong, Zurich, Washington, D.C., in a former tuberculosis sanatorium/monastery in the Adirondack Mountains, and elsewhere. He and his wife Ann Laemmle are now well settled in New York City.

Read more at paulwillcott.com.

www.ingramcontent.com/pod-product-compliance
Lightning Source LLC
Chambersburg PA
CBHW021442150726
47989CB00001B/358